Hindsight

Lessons learned from the Joplin tornado and other crisis events

by
Zac Rantz

with
Dr. Stephen Kleinsmith

Hindsight

Lessons learned from the Joplin tornado and other crisis events

Copyright © 2013 by Zac Rantz

Cover by: Kim Grimm Designs

Photos from Tracie Skaggs, Curtis Chesick, Zac Rantz, & Dreamstime.com

ISBN-13: 978-1494219291
ISBN-10: 1494219298

www.hindsightthebook.com
Email: info@zacrantz.com

Printed in U.S.A

DEDICATION

This book is dedicated to the Joplin community. Your ability to rise from the devastation is a testament to others that there is hope and that we have the ability within us to pick up the pieces and start again, no matter what we are faced with.

This book is also dedicated to my parents, family, and friends. You have supported me through my life and always encouraged me to follow my dreams.

And finally, this book is dedicated to my Lord and Savior. I know that You have given me a gift, and I hope that I am using it in a way to glorify You. As it says in Luke 12:46, "Much will be required of everyone who has been given much. And even more will be expected of the one who has been entrusted with more."

TABLE OF CONTENTS

INTRODUCTION

The stories and lessons that come in the following pages were compiled over laughter, tears, emails, and food the nights and weeks after the May 2011 Joplin tornado and in the days and years that have followed among friends and colleagues. When I started writing all of this, I never knew the journey that would follow with FEMA training, a hurricane, and other events that would show me how important it is to have crisis planning ingrained into all aspects of a school district.

Some of these things are what those of us who worked in Joplin talked about after taking time to reflect. Others are events that reinforced things, and experiences and revelations that showed changes that needed to be made in our own lives and school districts. Take these to heart. Chew on them, digest them, and see how they can apply to your school and life. We all have a crisis situation looming overhead, and, while we can't spend our lives in fear waiting for the rope to break and our lives to come crashing down, we can prepare, plan, and seek out ways to be ready. I hope and pray that you never experience a crisis that rips your life apart, but many of us will or already have.

I want to live my life with little or no regrets. I never want to know I could have done more but didn't take the opportunity to do so. We all know we need to be prepared, but often other things in life take precedence. Our school districts fight for time to complete all of the professional development needed in curriculum areas, but, if we can work to incorporate safety training into all areas, it becomes a part of the culture. As Aristotle said, "We are what we repeatedly do. Excellence, then, is not an act, but a habit."

When we ignore preparing, it becomes that small crack in the wall that you ignore, and, then, the wall falls apart and you wish you had addressed it when you first noticed it.

This is your opportunity. This is our opportunity. This is our chance to learn from events all around us. Many of these pages are filled with questions. These questions may lead to more questions. But, the answers lie with you and your school district. These are questions that have either never been asked or need to be asked again. These are quick thoughts and ideas that will hopefully be gold to you in preparing your district.

Those that have lived through crisis events want you to learn and want you to see what needs to be done to be better prepared. So, do it!

CHAPTER 1: MY GREATEST FEAR

I never imagined that one of my greatest fears would also present me with one of my greatest learning opportunities: tornadoes. In October of 1984, a tornado struck my dad's livestock feed and supply store. It was one of the weirdest memories I have, because I remember every-thing up to the point where the doors of the store flew open and my mom performed this ninja move to pull me under a desk. The next thing I remember is being at home with my aunt and needing a bath from the insulation that was ingrained in my clothing and hair.

Since that storm, I have had a horrible fear of tornadoes. I can remem-ber in kindergarten the sky turning pitch black and experiencing the feeling that I was going to be sick or pass out or something worse. I would just stare out the window, and my kindergarten teacher, Ms. Feldman, would have to refocus me away from the perceived threat outside.

My parents even worked with me to show me that the wind can do fun things through flying a kite so I didn't have worry and close my eyes and cover my ears every time the wind would blow.

Since something so uncontrollable happened, I then had to satisfy the need to control something. So, when a storm would develop, I would take all of my stuffed animals (pre-stuffed in a large, black trash bag) into my dad's closest where I would sit until the storm would pass.

As I grew up, the fear remained, and I would be anxious until a storm was over. I finally conquered my fear when the storm system that leveled Pierce City, Missouri, moved through the area and came over Nixa, which is about 50 miles east of Pierce City. I was a youth director at that time and all of the youth ministers had our students huddled in shelters and classrooms at the local Methodist church during a youth rally. Being the "responsible" youth directors, we went outside to see if we could see anything coming toward us from Pierce City. We had been warned the storm was coming, and as the clouds glided overhead and showed signs of rotation, a small funnel dropped, touched down, tossed up some debris, and then returned to the sky from which it came. And, I survived.

Since then, my fear has evolved into a fascination. Storm Chasers and other tornado shows engulf my attention. I would love to go storm chasing someday. I wanted to learn more (and still do) so I can somehow help others with this fear that took over my life for so many years.

And then May 22, 2011, came. When the initial reports of storms coming through the area developed, I was sitting at my home in Nixa. My interaction with Joplin had been minimal. I knew the city, but I had no real connection there other than knowing a few people who lived there.

As the warnings progressed, I heard reports that Joplin had been devastated, but I don't think anyone yet understood or could understand how bad it actually was.

When the warnings reached the neighboring county and they started sounding the sirens in Nixa, that anxious feeling surfaced. I rounded up my 80 pound beagle-boxer mixed dog and my school computer, and we headed toward the basement in my office.

I serve as the director of communication for Nixa Public Schools, so I knew that I would have to be at work if there was an emergency. Why

4

not be there and be ready?

I stood in the breezeway of my office watching the clouds, ready to dash downstairs if needed. As the storm approached, I watched the familiar green, tornadic sky that I saw in 1984, and so many times since, pass just south of me without inflicting much damage. I relaxed, and all returned to normal on that Sunday night.

Then a phone call on Monday morning took the week in an unexpected direction. I am a member of the Missouri School Public Relations Association (MOSPRA), and we are a close-knit group of school communication professionals. We all "get" each other and our jobs when others in our districts really don't understand what we do.

The call came from MOSPRA president, Jill Filer, asking for my assistance in Joplin as their school district had suffered significant damage from the Sunday night tornado. I immediately cleared it with my superintendent, and off I went to Joplin with my friend and counterpart from Ozark Schools, Curtis Chesick. I don't think either one of us was prepared for how our friendship would grow and develop over the coming days, but it is a bond that few will understand. We are a part of a family now. A family that has experienced the worst that nature can throw at a community and has seen what can happen in the hour of someone's greatest need.

CHAPTER 2: THE FIRST WEEK

I ran home and packed in about 10 minutes. You leave out a few things when you pack like that, but you don't realize it until right when you are ready for bed and need something. I also wish I would have thought more clearly about what to pack. But, I don't think I fully realized what I was going into and also how much a pair of work boots would have been my best friend those first couple of days.

I met Curt back at my office and off we went. We passed trucks and cars and vans, many of which were headed to Joplin. We could see that people had just collected what they thought was needed, like bottles of water or wood, and just left to go help. As we got closer to Joplin, we were guided in around the damage so we could actually get where we needed to go: the command center at Joplin North Middle School.

I really don't remember much of the conversation going over to Joplin. There had to be some Ozark and Nixa insult in there about how one school was better in some area than the other. Nixa and Ozark have a pretty intense rivalry that has existed for a good century. Curt and I harass each other often, but it's one of those "iron sharpens iron" friendships. We keep each other on our toes.

The hour-and-a-half trip to Joplin ended and, unbeknownst to me, a

Workers answer and make phone calls on Monday, May 23, 2011, from Joplin North Middle School.

new chapter of my life started when we walked through the doors of Joplin's North Middle School.

I will never, and I mean never, forget the zombie-like stare or overwhelmed look of those manning the command center. I can only wonder if I had the same look back in 1984. It's that look you get when you are so overwhelmed that you just go into robot mode and do what you need to do to function.

At that point in time, most hadn't slept for at least 24 hours. Many were dealing with damaged homes. Some no longer had homes, and others didn't know where family members were or if they had survived the horrific storm. But, here they were…working, doing what needed to be done for a school district and a community that needed them.

It's in a crisis that you see what people are made of. It was Shakespeare that wrote, "Some are born great, some achieve greatness, and some have greatness thrust upon them." Here was a group of people that did not choose to be in this situation. I know that there were days they all questioned why they were there. But, they were all placed there for a reason: pull Joplin out of the piles of rubble and make a place, a sanctuary, for the students to return to. Greatness was thrust upon them and they answered the call valiantly.

One thing Kim Vann, Joplin School's community development director, will tell you is that she would never just let a few people she barely knew, other than from our monthly MOSPRA meetings, come in and just take over her department. But she did. Curt, Tracie Skaggs (from the nearby town of Carl Junction), and I just ran with things and did what needed to be done. Looking back, one of the oddest things was how we just started getting things going and in place like it was all a part of a plan.

Our first task was to get some organization to the communications center. We were fresh blood, and we needed to come in and look at the situation with a new set of eyes and develop some system of organization so communication plans could function. Tracie had been there since just a few hours after the tornado (and continued to work all summer as well), but she was only one person in a sea of chaos.

So, Curt, Tracie, and I got some systems going and divided up what needed to be done and went to town. The Internet was down. Cell phone signal was spotty. And, we needed to get communication out. After some trial and error and a great deal of frustration, I did find out that the northeast corner of the library was where I could get the best cell phone signal to use my cell Internet card, but I had to hold up the computer at this weird angle in some odd yoga-like pose just to get it to barely work. So, I'd type a few emails and then go to the corner to send them.

Not too long after we showed up, Nicole Kirby from Park Hill, Missouri, arrived and got to work organizing as well. Nicole is always a voice of reason and logical thinking, which was needed in this situation. One of the main things we did was start communicating the list of needs or things that the district needed to do and try to help find out where the staff and students were. We were reaching out to the communities all around Joplin, because families had scattered after the tornado just to find shelter or get to or find relatives. Lists of media contacts, emails, and phone numbers were getting set up so that we could send out mass emails as needed. We basically had 7,700 missing students and over 1,000 missing staff members at that time because we didn't know where everyone was or how they were doing.

Facebook became our main communication tool since the school website was down. We asked people to post that they were okay so that some of the pressure on the four phone lines at the school would be relieved from trying to find and locate the students and staff members.

I noticed from some of my emails that were sent that first day that we were really focusing on people sending cash to help. Schools and organizations were rallying to help and they wanted to know what to do, so we said raise money. Joplin needed to be able to buy so much stuff (from pens and paper to computers and buildings) and having that money there to use was the best thing. They didn't need people dropping off things that could never be useful just to take up space, which was already happening. With half of the district's buildings damaged or destroyed, space was a luxury at that point in time and filling it up was not the best idea.

The day flew along as we tried to get some basic things like a printer and computers set up. And, we had just a "few" media calls to deal with (if you didn't, re-read the previous statement with the greatest sarcasm you can). In the midst of all of the other things going on, we were scheduling interviews with local and national media. But, this was the chance for Joplin Schools to tell its story. It was hit hard by this storm and people needed to know the story.

Let me insert a side-note here. In the middle of crisis where your computer systems and Internet are impacted, grab/hire/kidnap/bribe a technology person and keep him/her near you at all times. It will be

Hello this is your superintendent CJ Huff. During this sad and difficult time, we are trying to account for all of our students, faculty, and staff. If you have not notified the school through the Facebook page or have not been in contact with the district, please call 417-625-5270 to inform us of you or your children's status.

Please be patient and persistent when calling the school.

Additional information will be posted on the district's Facebook page as it is available.

Also, the public & faculty meeting at Memorial Education Center is canceled on Tuesday.

Our thoughts and prayers are with all of you during this difficult time.

Again, If you have not notified the school through the Facebook page or have not been in contact with the district, please call 417-625-5270 to inform us of you or your children's status.

The script of the rapid notification call made on Monday, May 23, 2011

like gold to you in a major situation like this.

One thing we needed to do was to start making contact with the students and staff in a way that they could hear Dr. CJ Huff's voice. CJ was their leader and hearing from your leader is needed in a crisis situation. It can both comfort them and also know that someone is in control. The only problem was that their rapid notification system was in the administration building that was hit by the tornado. They had managed to trek through the basement of the building and were able to download a student and staff list from the server so we had a spreadsheet of data to use, which was a starting point.

I was able to contact AlertNow (which is now called Blackboard Connect), which was the rapid notification service Nixa Public Schools uses. This was one of those times that I was happy that I had a service that works with you and not against you. I called in and a very nice man was on the other end. I cannot remember his name, but we talked several times those first few days and he was amazing help.

When I called into AlertNow, I think I gave them a two-minute speech that I was in Joplin, there was a tornado that took out their school's communication system, and we needed to use our system to send out

11

messages. Thinking I was going to have to do some convincing, I waited for a response to determine my next move. But, I got a friendly and calm, "let me see what I can do" on the other end of the phone.

Within five to ten minutes, we had Joplin set up on one of Nixa's accounts so the caller ID would show the Joplin phone number, and Dr. Huff was recording a message to send out. The message was going out and we thought things were good.

They, however, were not. You see, when you are in the middle of a crisis and cell phone signal is spotty, recording a message from a cell phone isn't a good idea. When the message was going out to the public, it was cutting off and not clear. Great! Just what we needed. So, about an hour later we were re-recording the message from a landline to be sent out again, this time a little clearer.

We completed a few more tasks that evening and then got ready to head down to the interviews that were scheduled for that night. I'll never forget CJ asking if he needed to change clothes before going on national media programs. Our response was "No." People needed to see the truth. They needed to see the superintendent in jeans and a polo who had been out all night and all day trying to put together some idea of what the school district looked like at that moment and what needed to be done for the students and staff.

As we got our evening schedule of interviews lined up, we all divided and conquered with different cars going to different interviews.

We were guided along the streets by CJ and Kerry Sachetta, Joplin High School principal, so we could get past the destruction and security check points. It was weird, because we could see where the edge of the tornado traveled. It was normal and then there was this strange line where the damage started.

I'll never forget that first moment when we were nearing the hospital. You could see the lights shining up into the sky from the hospital. The damage was bad, but when we crested the hill, it was like one of those

12

A picture of "satellite truck row" near the St. John's Hospital campus in Joplin.

war movies or some other "end of the world" type scene. It was just unreal. That picture is forever burned into my mind. People described it as a war zone, but Curt was the first to say that no war zone ever looked like this. It was more like someone had taken a massive lawn mower and driven it through the middle of town.

We made our way to "satellite truck row" down by St. John's Hospital to find the various TV stations that we were supposed to be interviewing with. We were to look for a white Skycom satellite truck. There were at least 10. Lovely. Oh, and did I mention it was pouring down rain and windy. Just one of many storms that rolled through the area that first week.

So, we finally found the CNN truck and tent and were told to wait and they would come and get us. When Curt got out of the SUV that first time, he had an umbrella. It was immediately turned inside out by the wind and broken. What do you do with a broken umbrella in the middle of a natural disaster? Just toss it on a pile of debris next to you.

So, we waited, and then they canceled the interview because it was too stormy. They didn't want to risk it. So we started to head back to our next interview when CNN called and wanted to do a phone interview. We had to quickly find a location that had cell phone signal and just

Assistant superintendent Angie Besendorfer waits inside the satellite truck before her interviewed on Fox News on Monday, May 23, 2011.

Dr. CJ Huff being interviewed by Fox News outside in the middle of a rain storm on Monday, May 23, 2011.

wait. So, we waited, and waited, and waited for CJ to be interviewed by Pierce Morgan. It was taking quite a while, so we had to move to make our way toward the Fox News truck (which was two down from the CNN truck we just left, but we didn't know it at the time because none of them were labeled).

As luck would have it, we were cut off and had to call back in. We were finally waiting for the interview and right when CJ started to go live, we lost signal again.

We called right back, but when we were put back on hold and could hear the program, it sounded like they were interviewing someone else and calling him CJ, so we don't know if there was a mix up or not. I still haven't seen that program to know what actually happened.

Well, we never made the CNN interview and had to hurry to the Fox News one. As luck would have it, a large band of rain moved in for the outdoor interview and the rain was just pounding CJ, but I've never seen a more honest and heart-felt interview than the one he gave there. He was still raw with emotion, and the world could see that. He gave

The front entrance to Joplin High School. The entry way has a steeple in it from the church that was across the street.

Joplin hope that night. He gave them a glimmer of what was to come.

Just to show you what kind of work the leaders in Joplin were doing, while all this was happening, Dr. Sachetta was in the Suburban on the phone trying to find the status of relatives in between the craziness of the interviews.

While the leaders were leading, they were also hurting and looking for their loved ones just like everyone else. This was true of many of the leaders in Joplin. Many of them had to turn off the personal part of their lives for a period of time and let the professional part take over so they could do what needed to be done.

As we left the interviews near the hospital campus, we tried to make our way back to North Middle School. However, since a tornado had come through, there was a lack of road signs. Needless to say, we were partially lost and ended up going the wrong way down a one way street because we thought we were on a different street. Piles of debris tend to look similar after a tornado, and since all of the landmarks were gone, it was a guessing game.

So, just picture us going down the wrong way and coming at us was the Missouri National Guard. They stopped us and we had to explain who we were and why we were there. We were just hoping that we didn't get arrested, because that would have been a great story to add to the situation. After checking on a couple of things, they cleared us to go.

We ended that night drenched and dropped everyone back off at North Middle School. CJ stayed the night there on the cot. He didn't really sleep, but he wanted to be there so things could get done if needed. We later found he really didn't really sleep for 66 hours. I still don't know how he functioned.

When we arrived at Tracie's house Monday night, I think our mental exhaustion was setting in as the adrenaline was wearing off. I honestly don't remember if I showered or not, but I had to have done that because we were drenched from the severe weather that night. I do remember how great the coolness of the leather couch felt after that long day. I think I just stopped, stared, and listened to the ceiling fan for a while.

That first night staying on Tracie's couch was odd. First, I didn't wake up that morning planning on being where I was. I remember just lying there trying to process the entire day. I had seen a lot that day, and I don't think my mind could fully grasp the level of destruction that I had seen.

The full scope had to be seen in the daylight, which would come the next day. We had seen pictures over and over again, but, as anyone who was there will tell you, until you saw it first hand and could just turn 360 degrees and just see the, well, flatness, the vastness of the destruction couldn't be fully understood.

Tuesday began with us going to Carl Junction to be able to work. We needed phone lines and Internet access that just weren't set up in Joplin. A group of us took over their school board room and called people, sent emails, and got more accomplished in about 30 minutes online than we had the previous day. After that morning, we broke off into groups to get our to-do list accomplished in Joplin. This included media interviews, state officials visiting, and many other things that would take too long to list.

Tuesday was also the first time I saw the high school. That image will stay with me forever. We were able to walk around and just look at the school while we waited for various people to arrive.

The vending machine that traveled down the hallway of Joplin High School.

I was able to see something that has changed my mindset forever, and after later seeing security footage from inside the school, it all made sense.

There was a vending machine right inside the doorway where the exterior doors of the school had been ripped off. The machine was sitting neatly up against the wall and looked to have been only slightly moved. I made the joke that tornadoes are interesting forces since it hadn't touched the machine but had ripped the doors off the school. I said that because of the random things I remember the tornado doing from when I was four, like picking up my dad's truck and turning it completely around and setting it back down or sucking out all of the cowboy hats but leaving other things in place.

This, however, wasn't the case at the high school. The vending machine was from the other side of the school and had traveled the entire length of the school, turned a corner, and been pushed up against a wall where it came to rest.

Curt and I went home that night. Mainly to see family and get a

The hallway that the vending machine traveled down in Joplin High School.

change of clothes (and more comfortable things like jeans and polos) since neither of us planned well the first time we left for Joplin. On the way back to Nixa and Ozark, we were still scheduling media interviews and prepping people for them.

In any crisis situation, you are going to have people who want to talk about what happened, but may not be able to. The communication professional's job is to make sure they are okay to talk and then help them talk through things. Being a school district, there are several regulations that are in place that prevent people from communication certain details because certain information legally cannot be talked about.

However, the school district needs to make sure it is talking to the media. Some media are great to work with. Others will take on tactics that aren't the most professional and can lead to inaccuracies being spread. For example, some media were calling whoever they could and verifying facts with wives or children of school officials. They were asking if certain people worked at the school or certain students went to school with them. The only problem with that is a student may have gone to the school at one point in time but could have moved and so the information the media is verifying isn't accurate, yet it gets reported as fact.

This is something that will not change no matter the crisis, so be prepared for it. David Cullen addresses this in his book *Columbine* when he addresses many of the things that were reported at the beginning of that school violence event that linger today…many of which were wrong. But in the quest to get the first information out many things will always be reported incorrectly, and, while they may be corrected later, they remain "fact" to people who may have never heard the correction.

On Wednesday morning, Curt and I left home about 3:00 a.m. to head back to Joplin. I had an interview with KY3, a Springfield, Missouri, news station, to talk about what was going on in Joplin Schools and update on what the district's focus was.

We arrived a little early, so we ran through McDonald's to grab breakfast. Since there was a boil-order in effect, there wasn't any coffee or ice or tap water, so we both ordered breakfast sandwiches and cans of soda to get us going that morning.

Once we made it to the interview location just east of the hospital, we parked and had a chance to take in the scene again. I'll never forget the smell of natural gas and freshly cut wood. And, above all, the eerie silence. It was too quiet. That was just a lack of life where there clearly should be.

That day and really the whole week was a blur. I've had to piece together certain events based on photos that were taken so I could see what I was wearing. I knew they happened, just not what day. There were press conferences, planning for dignitaries, working out systems and processes, and really just getting things running again in some form or another

After that week, it was back and forth between Joplin through vehicle, emails, and phone calls for the rest of the summer. MOSPRA had also organized response teams to come to Joplin for days and weeks, or in the case of Jim Dunn it was a year, at a time to work in the district's communication department. It was a team effort and really reinforced why it is important to have a network of people you can call on in a time of need. Our entire state's school public relations group rallied and helped staff the department over the summer. Some spent weeks or months or even the next year there helping out.

Kim and I also met for lunch several times just to talk. Sometimes it is just nice to get away from everything you are surrounded with for an hour or two just to talk about anything but the crisis. My friendship with Kim also taught me to surround myself with people who are there to support me, and this is needed even more in a crisis. In the middle of the dark, we all need friends to be a light. And Kim and I have been there for each other since that time for life's ups and downs.

I could go on and on with the stories, but more things are included in the following pages as I explain various events and things we all need to do. The main thing to do is prepare now and weave these lessons into our daily work practices so that when something happens we are as ready as we can be.

PART 1: PLAN

Notes:

CHAPTER 3:
WHAT ARE YOU PLANNING FOR?

What I find funny about everything we plan for is that we plan for the biggest and most horrific event that we think we could face, and usually it is reactionary to the event that just happened. Here lately it has been a gunman in our schools. Before that we were looking at tornado plans after Joplin and Moore, Oklahoma.

In all actuality, we should be planning for the day-to-day events. The chances of something catastrophic happening in our districts are fairly low when you think of the number of schools out there (around 100,000) and how many have been hit with something that made national attention.

In my district, the number one thing we plan for are student disruptions. After that, it is parents. Yep, we have to plan for the parent disruptions. Not a masked gunman. Your district may be different, but I think we all get lost in the major picture and don't focus on the day-to-day, which is what will help us be prepared when a crisis happens.

However, what is great about a plan is that if you do it right, the plan will translate to multiple situations. Too many times I've seen school districts trying to plan for every possible situation. I'm guilty of that. I mean, we had a plan for volcanic eruptions and my district is in Missouri. What you need to do is have a good structure and then work from that. Then, no matter what situation you have, you at least have a structure in place so you can begin to react.

If you try to plan for everything, you'll never get anything useful accomplished. If you have a good structure, everyone can know that.

So, plan for the big stuff, but don't overlook the day-to-day things. That is where your crisis plan will build a solid foundation.

What's funny is that we, many times, don't even ask what those day-to-day events are. One simple way to find that out is to survey your staff. They see things every day that are issues that the building or district administration might not even know about or think about. They see the holes and they can offer ideas.

There are many formal assessment tools out there, but a simple survey or email asking them what they see as potential hazards or crisis events will give you a great picture.

We now plan for power outages, loss of Internet, gas leaks, and other events that are a real possibility. In addition, we also plan for the fire, tornado, or active shooter.

A lot of those small things are what you will face in a major event, so that is a great place to start and where many things fall apart in the middle of a major crisis. Some of our individual buildings have other things they plan for since they are near places like a bank (robber running across school property) or a residential medial facility (patient escaping).

So, the real first question you should ask is "What do we need to plan for?", and then let that guide you in the process.

CHAPTER 4: FORM A TEAM

I never knew the value of a safety and security team until we formed one. Now, I won't ever be without one. Why? Well, first, let me tell you how to form one.

One of the biggest mistakes schools make is forming a safety team of just administration. This means you only get one perspective from the top level. You have to make sure you get people in the classroom, custodians, and clerical staff, in addition to the administration. Everyone sees each thing from a different point of view, and you need that when reviewing or addressing things. What might be a great idea from one perspective needs adjusting to fit another to work for the entire district. It really is a process of give and take to find the best solution.

We have the great fortune in Nixa to have a close relationship with our community. So, our safety team also has representatives from the fire department, police department, as well as other emergency management entities. We've kept it at about 15 people to be big enough to cover most areas, yet still be able to function as a team.

From there, we have advisory groups or members we contact on various issues. So, our transportation department, food service, student groups, parent groups, and various community groups are all a part of our expanded team.

Depending on your district and community, your team might look different. But, above all, you need varying viewpoints. A group that always agrees really isn't a group that will accomplish what needs to be accomplished.

Once you have your team formed, you need to go through training and other team-building events to really gain a sense of trust with each other. Our team took advantage of some national incident command training in Maryland that I think bonded us even more, that and we went through Hurricane Sandy.

Above all you need people who will come together to serve one purpose: the safety and security of students and staff.

Members from the Nixa Public Schools Safety and Security Team complete work during the Incident Command System training they received in Emmitsburg, Maryland, at the Emergency Management Institute.

CHAPTER 5:
REVIEW WHAT YOU CURRENTLY DO

One of the biggest mistakes some schools do when developing crisis plans it throwing out everything they are doing. There is a reason why you are doing some of the things you are doing, so figure that out.

As we have been reviewing and revising our plans in Nixa, we were looking at what some of our schools were doing. When we did that we found a lot of great ideas to implement district-wide. We were also able to see where schools were in their planning processes and help develop certain benchmarks to achieve for each building.

We also were able to get a district-wide picture of where we were. What did a certain drill look like in one building? Where we all doing different things?

During this review, we were able to find some areas that needed changing. One of those was the use of code words. One of the first things that our local emergency personnel told us to do was get rid of code words. Clearly stating what is happening over the intercom or in a message will allow people to react appropriately. Saying "code eagle's nest" over the intercom really didn't do much for the situation except to confuse people.

We also were able to see some great examples of evacuation plans that we implemented across the district. The school had it down and we just needed to adjust a few things to make it broad enough to fit the entire district. Why reinvent what is already done well?

The other thing we quickly realized is that we practice under ideal circumstances. The principals are in their location right when the drill starts so they can monitor things. However, that is not likely to happen when an actual event happens. People will be spread out all over the building and will have to travel to get their assigned places. You need to practice that in some way just to work through any issues that could arise.

So, take a few moments to see what is already going on or not going on and you'll get a good idea of your starting point.

CHAPTER 6:
DEVELOP/REVISE YOUR CRISIS PLAN

One of the first things that an organization needs to do is have some sort of a plan. Now, this plan will be adjusted and some of it may be thrown out the window depending on the situation, but you need a plan. Why? Well, in a crisis situation when people do not know how to react or when rational thinking has gone out the window, having something that people can use as a guide will repay you multiple times the amount of time you put into developing it.

There are many types of crisis plan materials. The National School Public Relations Association's (NSPRA) Crisis Communication manual is a good one. This manual is what we worked from in a lot of situations during my time working with Joplin. There are handouts and things in there that are gold when you have no idea what to do. By taking that manual and adapting it to fit into other Community Emergency Response Team (CERT) plans with your local, county, and state governments, you will have a plan that will function as the backbone in your crisis.

However, any plan is not a good tool unless it is rehearsed before a crisis. Simply waiting to pick it up until a crisis happens will not benefit anyone. If you haven't practiced the plan enough prior, it will be like you didn't have a plan at all.

While you are planning, you will need to assign clearly defined roles to staff that will be a part of the district and building crisis teams. This should be done in advance as a part of the plan, and those roles should have clear expectations and requirements so that the positions or jobs can be functional quickly in a crisis. You will also need to have back-ups for each position so that if people are not able to perform their du-ties, someone else is able to step-in easily. Then, you need to practice those roles. Table-talk discussions are a great way to just get people thinking about what they need to do and whom they need to call.

You will also be able to think through various situations prior to a crisis. I never thought about the scenario of what to do when someone wants to donate one million dollars to your relief efforts. Where does it go? Do the people in charge under the superintendent know what to do if he/she can't make decisions? What happens in your schools when the principal is out? Is there someone designated to make deci-sion in a crisis that has the knowledge to make informed decisions? And, have you equipped staff to know enough of the building or dis-trict to step in wherever they may be needed?

Because a district can be overwhelmed in a crisis, it is also a good idea to consider having some positions in your district have backups or mutual aid agreements outside of the district or at least have people who are familiar with how systems work so they can help out. Many times districts have one person in a department (like communication, technology, human resources, your business office, etc.), and those de-partments need backups, too. The disaster in Joplin showed the need for people who can take over as needed. When your key people are incapacitated in some manner, you still need to be able to function.

After you've asked a lot of questions and talked through various situ-ations and have your plan completed, it should not just sit on a book-shelf or never be touched again. Since experiencing this disaster, I have taken more notes and have more ideas than I know what do with. My district's crisis plan will change and evolve because of Joplin and other events around the country.

You will need to review your crisis manual multiple times a year and make adjustments as needed. Things change frequently in an organization, a city, and in the country, and your crisis manual needs to as well. This needs to be a living, breathing document that is reviewed and practiced often. Yeah, that's right. You need to practice it. Your manual is nothing more than a paperweight in a crisis if people do not know what is in it or how it works. Practicing can range from life-like drills to tabletop discussions. But, you need to practice it and know it. You'll wish you had if you don't.

You will also want to consider having your partner school districts or organizations know how your crisis plan works. Before our Joplin experience, my counterpart in Ozark, Missouri, Curtis Chesick, and I were familiar with how each other worked in our respective districts, so we knew what each other's crisis plans were, to a certain extent.

Now, this will change, and we will share additional information and additional plans with each other so that if a crisis hits we will both be ready to assist. This continues to evolve as we also use the same type of planning structure so both districts are speaking the same crisis planning language. What is great is that both districts are using the same structure for our crisis plans, so we don't have to know all of the specifics because the structure is the same.

Consider having regular meetings with people you would work with in a crisis. People from local hospitals or other organizations that you would be directly interacting with would be good people to invite to lunch just to make sure the first time you are talking is not in the middle of a crazy event.

By the end of the first week in Joplin, Curt and I were on the same wavelength with a lot of decisions. This came from knowing how we were going to operate and following the same plan. Notice a theme here? Plan, practice that plan, involve those who need to know the

33

plan, and then practice it with them.

As a part of that plan, you need to have several letters, statements, or anything else you might need for crisis communication pre-written with blanks. As terrible as it sounds, the last thing you want to be doing in the middle of a crisis is trying to write a sane, logical letter or even a death statement. It's a horrible thought, but you have to prepare for something like that. You need to do it at a time where you are not emotionally attached to the situation.

Take these letters and statements and store them in several places like flash drives or cloud systems. Make sure that you keep a record of where these documents are stored so you can update them regularly when your crisis manual is updated.

I like the idea of a cloud system that way you update them in one location where several people can access them, but you also need to be prepared for the lack of Internet (which will be addressed later on). NSPRA's manual does have a large collection of statements and letters, but you will have to add some that are specific to your district.

Chunk It Out

When you are in the process of developing or revising your plan, developing a series of benchmarks or steps to complete along will not only help make sure that everyone has the same parts of the plan completed, but it will also make it more digestible to your buildings with everything else they are required to do. Some things will have to come all at once, but where you can, roll it out in manageable chunks.

Consider having monthly "Safety in Six" talks at administrator meetings or monthly tasks for people to complete as you are developing or revising parts of your plan.

These monthly updates are also a good time to keep people on the same page as to where you are in the process and what they can expect in the future. No one likes to caught off guard, so the more you can communicate, the better it will be for your district.

Mutual Aid Agreements

One of the hardest things to do is ask for help, especially in a crisis situation. You are trying to gain control of the situation, and you might not even think to ask for help until it is way past the time of needing it.

So, before a crisis even happens, develop mutual aid agreements with other school districts, superintendents, businesses, etc. These people either need to call you and see if you need help, or if the situation warrants, just show up.

This is part of the success of the communication efforts during the tornado. The Missouri School Public Relations Association (MOSPRA) along with assistance from the Kansas School Public Relations Association (K-SPRA), the Oklahoma School Public Relations Association (OK-SPRA), NSPRA, and other communication professionals all worked to assist Joplin Schools with its communication efforts.

As I mentioned before, when Curtis and I walked into the district's command center, we were greeted with a bunch of overwhelmed and exhausted (both emotionally and physically) people. These people were not only trying to run a school district, but many of them were digging themselves out of a pile of rubble or searching for missing friends and family. So, we just started doing what we were trained to do.

Kim Vann, Joplin School's Director of Community Development, has stated time and again that she would never turn over her program and department to anyone before this, but because of the professional relationship she had with us prior to the crisis, she knew that Curtis, Tracie, and I could be trusted and just let us run with it. She is one brave woman for that.

As Curtis and I were working with Tracie, the three of us divided and conquered and worked as one entity throughout the rest of the week (and even off and on in different capacities throughout the summer).

Why is all of this important? Well, for one, anyone going through a crisis is going to need a fresh set of eyes. Sometimes we are blinded and overwhelmed by the situation. We also need someone rational on hand. You need someone who is objective who can help talk to you about and through decisions. This is why it is important to have another communication person or administrator who you can call or have there.

In a crisis the size of the Joplin tornado, you are going to need an expanded communication program, so having communication professionals on call until you can fill their positions more permanently will serve you well.

Curtis and I are in the process of developing mutual aid agreements with our surrounding districts and emergency organizations so that we are all on the same page and can assist each other as needed, no matter what the crisis is. MOSPRA also plans on working to make this a regional or statewide effort as a resource to each other. After all, you can't handle a crisis all on your own. Just having someone to call in a situation for advice will be golden in the middle of a situation. And, in order to call them, you'll need some contact information. Keep that information handy and stored in a few places. Your cell phone may be gone when you need it most.

This is even true in our personal lives. If something happens the size of Joplin, which could be a hurricane, wildfire, earthquake, or snow/ice storm, it might be a smart idea to have people outside of the area with some of your information or at least copies of your plan so you can access it if you need it.

CHAPTER 7:
PLAN TO WORK WITH THE MEDIA

In the middle of a crisis, you have to have a little fun. The world may be falling apart, but you have to keep your sanity. So, my friend and communications counterpart, Nicole Kirby, and I decided to have our little media geek-out moment and see if through the course of all the craziness in Joplin, we would happen to run into Anderson Cooper. I mean people have their favorite sport stars, musicians, or actors, why can't communication people have our stars? So, if we were out and about and we met him, it would be an exciting time. If not, no love lost. So, in the craziness of the week and after attending and planning numerous press conferences, there was no encounter with Anderson Cooper at that point. I did have instructions to say "Hi" to Brian Williams for another friend, but, alas, neither one had crossed our paths.

Now there are only so many press conferences one can go to. So, I decided to take a break and miss one. It was Wednesday and it was just going to be another one like the day before, and I already knew parts of what they were going to say, so it wouldn't hurt to just take a break and get some work done. So I stayed at North Middle School to get some work done. In the middle of answering some emails and completing some paperwork, I received a text. This text was a picture. This picture was of someone standing right next to the people that went to this press conference from the Joplin Schools communication

The picture of Anderson Cooper that was texted to me from the press conference that I decided not to go to.

department. This person was…say it with me now…Anderson Cooper. So, the moral of the story is, never, never, ever, ever miss a press conference or you will be punished!

I tell you all this because working with the media is something I really love doing. We are all in this game together. Schools have stories we want told. The media have stories that they want to report. When we work together, great things happen. And that is why the media can be your best friend or your worst enemy in a crisis. Their job is to communicate information and your job is to provide them with information. How you do that outside of a crisis will translate how you do that in a crisis.

In Nixa, we have an open and honest relationship with the media, and that two-way trust allows us to work well with our local media. In a crisis situation, they know how we will communicate and what to expect from us. But, in a crisis the size of the Joplin tornado, you'll be interacting with your local media as well as national and maybe international media. The national media won't always care or want to follow your pre-designed communication procedures, so you need to be prepared for that.

For example, we received a call that a national media organization was ignoring the "No Trespassing" signs and exploring Joplin High School with a camera crew. We only knew about this and they only asked permission to be there after they had been filming for a while because they ran into a school official.

Like I stated before, you will also find that media outlets will call homes of various school employees and "verify" facts with spouses or children that do not work for the school district. It is then that you realize that you have to have some control over what is happening.

As the days in Joplin progressed, we were more proactive in reaching out and making contact with the various news agencies to help control some of the rogue reporters. We were able to prove our ability to get them what they needed and help them produce good stories. Many of them saw us as a part of the team rather than someone with whom they were in competition.

Limited People Speak In The Beginning

Now, for those that know me, I am one of the biggest proponents of open and honest communication. And, I'm not saying that should change. But, in the middle of a crisis, and really at the beginning of a crisis, you need to be as in control of your message as possible. When a school official speaks, those words get reported and once things are out there, it is hard to get them changed. Just think about the Facebook status or message that gets spread around or those emails that get forwarded even when they have been found to be false. What is said in a crisis will go viral quickly.

So, why really rein in your people? Well, we were trying to find out the truth and the truth was changing a lot as more details were received. We didn't know who had been killed, who was missing, what the extent of some of the damage was, and a whole host of other details. When people from the school start talking, they are viewed as experts, and what they say will be what gets reported. I have friends

39

in the media who have expressed to me that they feel that the media should be allowed to go out and get their story. I completely agree. But, in the midst of a lot of unknowns, your spokesperson should be the main speaker and then everyone else should be cleared through the communication office so they know what the facts are.

It is important that you communicate this out to all of your staff. Just let them know what they should do with media calls in the event of an emergency or crisis. Then make sure that you have a system in place to handle the media calls. Have numbers and information posted on your website so when people search, it is easily found. You should also have conversations with them about posting things on social media. They may not view it as such, but they are making a statement that cannot be easily erased and could be horribly inaccurate, but since that person is a school employee, it becomes more official than if someone else made it.

In Joplin, the superintendent or district official making a public statement would be in contact with or come by the communication office before he or she spoke just so we could verify facts and make sure that everyone was on the same page. Dr. Huff might have made some decisions or the communication office might have learned something new. By staying in contact, we could verify facts on both sides. That way, when a message was released to the public or questions were answered at a press conference or through phone calls, things were as factual as that moment allowed.

It was also important to know who was being interviewed so that we could brief them on what was factual. Curtis and I were talking with people who were getting ready to be interviewed while we were driving, well he was driving and I was talking, because we had to give them the most up-to-date information five minutes before they were interviewed. We also needed to make sure they were fit to be interviewed. In a crisis situation, people's emotions are raw and while the media may want an interview with someone, it is the communication

The statement that was released at the beginning of the first week after the tornado to the media and public regarding Joplin School's ability to comment on the status of the students and staff.

professional's duty to protect them, and, if they aren't ready, we have to say no and move to someone else. Many times people think they are ready, but they aren't.

I realized this in a different incident when a student in Nixa died and the media wanted an interview with different people. Some thought they were ready, but as they were getting ready to be interviewed, they just couldn't do it. They were too raw at the moment.

Another issue will be things like FERPA (Family Educational Rights and Privacy Act) or other privacy laws, which limits what information school districts can legally release. Make sure that what you say and what you do does not violate these laws. Each state will have different laws and each district has different policies, so it is important that you know what you can and cannot do ahead of time. You need to know what you can and cannot confirm about a student or employee when people call (this might be a good check list to have in your crisis plan). This is invaluable knowledge for you to know this like the back of your hand for everyday media requests as well as requests in a crisis situation involving student and staff information.

We had a student in Nixa who was involved in a car accident on the way to school. Because this student was a minor, the district could not release information; you have to adhere to privacy laws. These laws allow the superintendent to release information in an emergency but only to "appropriate parties," but it has to be approved by the superintendent to release that information and that information must be need-

41

Joplin Schools
Press Pass

By order of the Joplin R8 School District,

_____

is permitted to enter restricted areas in order to conduct communications business for the Joplin Schools.

_____
Superintendent Dr. CJ Huff

The press pass that was issued to media to help them access various school sites around Joplin.

ed in accordance with the law's provisions, not just because someone wants it. You can't confirm or deny things that the law doesn't so be clear on these provisions, or have your school lawyer on call when this happens. I do have to say a special "thank you" to Kelli Hopkins in the legal department at the Missouri School Boards' Association for her assistance and guidance with all of these legal issues. She was and will continue to be a great resource. Make sure you have a resource like her now so you can call that person when you need information or guidance.

There are also other instances that can prevent you from saying certain things. You will want to make sure that you are cleared to give out information by contacting the local emergency management or law enforcement. I hate to make things worse, but in a disaster, it is not uncommon to make sure that those who have died were killed because of the storm and not someone taking advantage of the situation, so you have to make sure that the district confirming the person's death is not a part of an ongoing investigation. This is also true if a student or employee has died. You have to make sure that people don't open their mouths before they should. Having these statements cleared through the communication office is a great practice. Just make sure that the communication office is talking to the right people (law enforcement

Assistant superintendent Angie Besendorfer speaks at one of the joint press conferences held by the city, school, and county.

as well as legal advisors) to have what the school is going to say approved.

As the situation in Joplin evolved, the communication office relaxed, but it was important to still keep control of our message. In your district, make sure everyone understands they are not to speak unless cleared by the communication department/central office. In the middle of a crisis, it is better to have a tight control and then relax that rather than trying to chase and correct what people have been saying on their own.

Limit People Speaking For The District

Why do you want one person as the spokesperson for the school district? Well, there are two reasons for this. First, you want to have the superintendent viewed as a leader and the person who is in control of the situation. This is the same for a city or business. It is not a coincidence that in President Obama's speech on the death of Osama Bin Laden that there were a lot of "I" statements. He was in control and the speech was written to show that he was the one that was handling the situation. This should be the same for the superintendent. In the middle of a crisis, people look for a leader. Dr. Huff was an amazing one. He told people what they needed to know. He let them know he was in control of the situation. And, he gave them goals and told them how they could help meet those goals.

The second reason you want limited people speaking is because of the craziness of the situation. One person speaking is a lot easier to manage than a whole group. This of course will change as you go throughout the crisis, but, at the very beginning, the number of people speaking should be limited.

For your district it might be most appropriate to have your one spokes-person doing interviews and the public information officer/communications professional holding other press conferences to distribute facts. Also, you might have your communications professional doing regular updates and then have a time for interviews with your superintendent or district official. Then, as soon as you can, open it up for more people to speak. We worked to increase the number of people speaking quickly to include principals and some other staff members, but we briefed them all before their interviews so they knew what they could and couldn't say. We still kept the communication office releasing facts and doing those updates to the media, but we were able to show the various sides of the tornado by allowing people to speak from various perspectives.

Distribute Fact Sheets

Since things in a crisis are constantly changing, and in a disaster the scale of Joplin, there is so much information to digest, you need to provide the media and the public with a time-stamped fact sheet. This will keep your information out there and people can reference it if needed. It also helps prevent misinformation (there will still be that, but this will help) as the media and public reference the sheet. It is also important to have it time and date stamped so that if you send one

The fact sheet that was distributed on May 26, 2011, to the media and public updating them on various facts and information about the Joplin Schools tornado recovery efforts.

out in the morning and then have to update it, people can reference the newer of the two.

After things slowed in Joplin we interviewed the media to get feedback. Many stated they would like a fact sheet earlier in the day. We were in the habit of sending it out in the afternoon, but many stated that it would have been nice to have it earlier when possible. The media have deadlines and we need to work with them to make sure those deadlines are met with the most accurate information we can provide. It would have been better for us to distribute a fact sheet earlier in the day so the media could shoot their story and then make adjustments before it aired if anything was updated. This would have been easier than us distributing the fact sheet later in the afternoon which would cause them to scramble to figure out how they would cover the updated information.

It is also a good idea to provide the media and public with a copy of the superintendent's speech. Many will want to quote it, so having it available is a benefit for them. It will also help in case the audio didn't work well and they need to know what was said. This will help reduce a misquotation or the reporting of misinformation.

Have Clear Guidelines To Give To The Media

As stated before, a crisis will be chaotic. You cannot avoid that. You can control how things are handled. The media will be its own situation. If a large crisis happens (this can be from a tornado, to an abuse scandal, to a controversial board decision), you need to set guidelines for the media. You have this right as a district to specify media interactions, and you should use it when needed. You need to do this to protect your students and staff. Joplin was the perfect case for this. The media need to know if they are allowed on school property, which property they can come to, what they can film, who they can film, and what you will and will not give them. This might sound harsh, but this allows them to know what they will and will not get. Some of this is also based on legal issues and you just can't provide them with information. Don't waste their time. It is precious and should be respected.

For example, until we found every staff member and student, the district was not going to comment on any individual's status. There were

MEDIA DIRECTION FOR SCHOOL OPENING ACTIVITIES
Joplin School
August 11, 2011

The American "can do" spirit is alive and well in Joplin, Missouri. Joplin Schools will open for students Wednesday morning, August 17. In just 86 days, entire schools have been created from places such as warehouses, an old shopping mall box store and a retired school building. Thousand of students, teachers and parents gathered for a community memorial for an emotional look back last Wednesday, August 10. Lost students and staff will always be remembered. The new day starts Monday.

Opening Day Celebration (Aug. 15, Monday)
An opening day convocation and rally for staff and teachers is slated for Monday, August 15, 8:00 am at Taylor Performing Arts Center on the Campus of Missouri Southern State University. Following the rally teachers and staff will return to buildings to prepare for the first day of class.

Tuesday is Volunteer and Preparation Day (Aug. 16, Tuesday)
All schools will be bustling with activities August 16 as staff and volunteers put the finishing touches on schools, busses and support facilities.

Wednesday, Schools Open (Aug. 17, Wednesday)
86 days earlier, Superintendent Huff astonished the city by announcing that schools would start as planned on August 17. The fulfillment of that promise is major cause for celebration in Joplin Schools. Superintendent C.J. Huff will visit every elementary school to have an individual picture taken with each new Kindergarten student.

We welcome your arrival
and are thankful for the opportunity to tell our story.

To facilitate media requests and ensure the safety of students, please comply with the following:

- Please have your media badge clearly on display at all times and hand a copy of your card to everyone you interview.

- All visits to school property and interviews with Joplin Schools students and employees must be coordinated through the Communications office, 417-625 5202 ex. 2224 or jdunn@joplin.k12.mo.us. (you will have the opportunity for interviews, we just need to know who is in our buildings and make sure student identities are protected as prescribed by law).
- Superintendent C.J. Huff will be available for the media Monday, Tuesday and Thursday from 1:00 PM to 2:00 PM for interviews at the Administration Building.

The media were welcomed into Joplin for the opening day of school on August 17, 2011, but they were given clear guidelines on what was expected of them in order to keep some structure to the day as well as protect the students and staff who were coming back to school, many of which would be seeing each other for the first time since the tornado struck.

47

- Superintendent Huff, students, teachers, and administrators will be available for interviews at the 10th – 12th grade building at 2:30 PM on the first day of school.
- Assistant Superintendent Angie Besendorfer will be available after the Rally on Monday, August 15

Here are opportunities to connect with teachers, principals, students, parents and administrators for exclusive interviews.

Monday: After the Rally (11-noon) at Walker Perfoming Arts Center on the campus of MSSU. See interview with Angie Besendorfer above.

Tuesday: 2:00-4:00 p.m., 11th and 12th grade Center; 101 Rangeline, Joplin MO

Wednesday 2:30-4:00 p.m., 11th and 12th grade Center; 101 Rangeline, Joplin MO

Please do not approach parents and students on school grounds with questions without advance permission from the Communications office or the principal's office. School policy forbids being in schools without an escort or direct permission from the Communications office. Please do not capture student faces in video or photographs without parent or school district consent.

Early Morning Shows August 17 at the 11th and 12th Grade Facility
In order to accommodate busses, student drivers and drop-off vehicles, we must keep the front of the school open. We will provide space for media trucks. A wide variety of people will be available for interviews starting at 5:30 a.m. We hope to be able to accommodate specific requests by scheduling in advance.

THANKS YOU FOR COVERING OUR STORY!
We will do everything in our power to help you cover this important story. We appreciate your cooperation in making this day special for our students, teachers and staff.

too many unknowns, and we just made sure that we were not going to comment. It was also not the district's place to confirm deaths or injuries. Laws prevent that to a certain extent, and things were changing so much that much of what the district was hearing needed to be confirmed. In many cases, until the family or law enforcement has released information, you can't say anything about it.

When the district had a back-to-school celebration for the students, limited media access was given to allow the students to have a chance to interact with each other privately, which for many was the first time they had seen each other since the tornado struck. The district worked to get students and staff for the media to interview, but we also worked to protect the students.

We also had the issue of people (not just the media) going onto school property and into school buildings that were not safe. We didn't know if they were looters, students, or just random people, so when we got calls that people were in buildings, the district had to respond. This wasted time that could have been spent other places. Having clear guidelines will help keep people safe and the situation clear for everyone. You have to remember that it is the district's property and you should be clear who is and is not allowed on it.

These guidelines can change depending on the situation or where you are in the crisis. But, you need to have clear guidelines on whom they call, what can and cannot be done, and who can be interviewed.

Local vs. National Media

As just about any PR person knows, there is a major difference between the local and national media, and you will have to work with those differences in a crisis. In most crisis situations, you will not have to deal with national media, but you may have to deal with more regional media from a larger or different market than yours. You have relationships (I didn't say good or bad) with your local media and those relationships will continue long after the regional or national media have gone, so don't ever lose sight of the fact that you will need to make sure to take care of the local media's needs. However, the national and regional media do carry power to get your story out in a way that the local media never could. So, don't ignore them.

These are important things to know:

1. In a major crisis situation, events are going to be long-term stories.

    *   The focus will change over time and you need to be prepared for that. The beginning of a crisis will be a time when people are looking for facts. After that, the story focus will move more into the individual focus and putting a face on the

event. You need to anticipate when these changes are starting to occur so that you can adjust how you are preparing for the news stories.

- In a case like Joplin, you need to plan for the future. There will be lots of firsts after a major crisis that will be covered. The first day of school, first sporting event, first homecoming, first graduation, first prom, etc. These will all be covered in some way and you will need to prepare for that.

- Be prepared to monitor media coverage. You need to know what is being reported and work to make sure the truth stays out there when things are reported incorrectly. We live in the age of quick information, and in many instances that information is wrong, but it still gets reported. So, when this happens, you will need to work to correct the rumor, find where it started, and see if you need to go to the source to stop it from being repeated.

- It is important that someone is assigned to monitor media coverage. You will need to know what is being said, and having someone focused on that is a major benefit. This should not be your main PR person, though. They will need someone to do this for them and keep them informed of what is being said and reported. This duty rotated to different volunteers and other PR people helping out in Joplin, but we did our best to make sure people were monitoring what was being said.

2. Local media might be impacted by the event so your focus might be more on regional and national media. This was the case in Joplin. They had to bring in additional reporters from outside of the area to help out since many media members lost homes or had friends and family missing. You could be dealing with people who have little to no history of the area and will need more background information at times just to be clear on the situation. Make sure and

you take time to give them this background information because it will improve the quality of the story they write if they understand the situation better. One of the main reporters we worked with was a sports reporter from another market that came down to help.

3. Have a media contact list printed and posted. This list should include phone numbers of district people who will speak on different topics, newsroom phone numbers, and other important reference numbers. You will refer to this list more times than you can count and will not want to have to open it on your computer each time. This way you know who the point person is for various topics that you know will come up. Then, be prepared to expand the list as more topics develop that the media will want to conduct interviews on.

4. As I addressed in the story of working in Joplin, one thing you need to realize and plan for in the beginning is the fact that the media will more than likely get facts wrong, especially in the beginning. In the age of 24-hour news, there is a lot of down time between press conferences and other updates, so they have to fill airtime or their social media with content.

   What results is a lot of speculation or grasping at any kind of source they can find. This happened in the Columbine school shooting and it happened in the Boston bombings. It is a fact and should be prepared for. While this is something that the media needs to work on with reporting, it is also just going to be a fact. Plan for it. They are only human and are trying to do their job of finding facts. The more information you are able to supply them the more accurate the information they distribute will be.

5. As I stated above, you need someone monitoring media coverage. You might also need a separate person monitoring social media as well. It just depends on the size of the event or how much it is being shared on social media. Once false information is out there on social media, it will get shared and you will plan for what will

This is the international press conference held in the library at Joplin Middle School on Wednesday, May 25, 2011. Area superintendents game to Joplin for the press conference to stand behind Dr. Huff to show their support of Joplin.

seem like an endless job of correcting things. Just think of those false stories or "news" from websites that gets shared daily on social media. It will be much worse in the middle of a disaster.

Press Conferences:

Press conferences will be a vital tool in a crisis. You will need to have a plan for these and have a checklist developed that you can hand to someone to complete. In Joplin's situation, people outside of Central Office were helping and having a list of things for them to set up allowed for easy planning. You will need things like a sound system, podium, and a generator if you are going places without power (like one of the damaged schools), and a backdrop of some kind. Remember that the media need a visual for their story when possible. The backdrop could be a destroyed school building or the command center in the background. It could also be a group of volunteers or superintendents that have come to show support. No matter what the case, they need a good visual.

The media did request that we try to hold our informational press

Melanie Dolloff works on the grid that was used to organize national and local media interviews on the first day back to school in Joplin in August 2011.

conferences in a joint conference with the other organizations involved in the recovery efforts. The district worked with the city and county to accommodate that. Then when we had special events or other school specific announcements, we held our own. These would be to announce things like the rebuilding effort and the construction efforts at different buildings.

When planning your press conferences at different buildings or locations, do keep in mind that travel time and schedules might prevent the media from making it. If it is a community crisis, try to work to make sure you don't conflict with other press conferences or announcements.

No matter what the situation, try to have one location for all of your press conferences. Make sure it is functional and easy to get to (as much as you can) for both staff and the media. Your job is going to be to communicate information and reducing the roadblocks to that will help you do that more effectively.

A Joplin teacher is interviewed in front of the new 11th and 12th grade center at the Northpark Mall on the first day of school in Joplin on August 17, 2011.

Organize Those Who Are To Be Interviewed:

Having a daily schedule of who is available for interviews and when they are available and setting that up in some sort of grid or chart will help with your scheduling. Jim Dunn, a fellow Missouri PR professional, implemented this while he was helping out in Joplin, and it was an amazing tool to have. Divide the grid up into 15-minute segments. Most basic interviews take that long, and you can always block off more than one segment. It is also a good practice to email media outlets on major events and give them instructions on how to schedule interviews for that day.

This grid became very handy on the first day of school when media outlets descended on Joplin again and wanted interviews beginning at 5 a.m. throughout the rest of the day. And, just because you are organized doesn't mean all of them will be. Many will show up and need to interview someone, so the chart helps a lot in those circumstances. It is also good to have a pool of students, parents, and staff on hand. One thing the media hates is having the same person to interview as another news network (unless it has to be that one person). So, when you have big events, have multiple people and try to keep the number of times the people in that pool are interviewed equal so the same person doesn't pop up on every news outlet when it could have easily been any other person doing that interview. This is a good practice to implement on regular news stories in your district.

The satellite news trucks sit in front of the new 11th and 12th grade center at the Northpark Mall at 4:30 a.m. on the first day of school in Joplin on August 17, 2011.

CHAPTER 8:
COMMUNICATION TOOLS NEEDED

If you are going to build a house, you need some basic tools: a hammer, a drill, a screwdriver, and a construction crew. Communication in a school district or organization is no different. You need your basic "tools" and then you need your "crew." You wouldn't try to build a house without the right tools, so why do we try to function as a communication department without the right equipment?

Before a crisis hits, you need to know what tools you have, how they are used, and make a list of them. Why? Well, when you aren't thinking clearly in a crisis, you have a list of resources already developed and can use the list to make sure you are using everything at your disposal. You can also use those as a checklist on what is operational and what is not.

The checklist should include all of the ways you will send out information from your social media, to e-newsletter, to website, to text alerts, to posting flyers on bulletin boards around town. Don't forget to include the basics, because you might forget about those. Having a calling tree on your checklist might be the one thing that you would have forgotten about, but it might be one of the only things functioning. We moved away from a calling tree, but we have a staff directory that can be divided up easily to contact staff if needed. You also need a list of key community people that need to be notified. These lists need to be off-site and not just on your cell phone.

It is also important to have communication/media contact phone numbers listed on all school websites and on Facebook pages where they can be easily accessed or found. In a crisis, the media will be calling. You want them calling you. Make sure they know where to go and how to get in touch with you.

After experiencing the crisis in Joplin, the following communication tools are things you need to have or consider having in your district.

A Rapid Notification System

One of the major tools of the Joplin crisis was a rapid notification system that was off-site. The district did have a dialer that was on-site, but the storm took it out of service, so we had to use Nixa's system since it was off-site until theirs was back up and running. I know that in the middle of budget cuts, you have to make choices, but this should not be something you skimp on. You'll regret it if you do when you have a crisis situation.

One other lesson we learned was to make sure the calls to the customer service line were made from a landline phone if possible or email them the script so they can record it. As was said before, one of our first calls was made from a cell phone and the signal was spotty and the message didn't record well, which led to more confusion when the message was sent out.

What should you look for in a rapid notification system?

1. A system that has multiple call data centers across the US. That way, if they all go down, the crisis is probably bigger than your district and sending out a message really won't be necessary.

2. A system that is located off-site. There are some systems that have both off-site and on-site components. However, you need to make sure you have an off-site component to be able to call all of your

families if your on-site system goes down.

3. A system that has great, 24-hour customer service. When we called AlertNow/Blackboard Connect, they didn't hesitate to help us use part of Nixa's account to work for Joplin. I told them what I needed and it was done within five minutes and we were making calls within 10 minutes (we had to write the script and load the student information or it would have been done faster).

   We were calling at night to schedule calls because the phone lines were more open then. We needed someone at the company's office who could record the call over the phone and send it for us because we were without good Internet service. Make sure the company you use has 24-hour access and great customer service. If they don't, you'll wish you were with a company that did while in the middle of your crisis.

4. A system that can call, text, email, and maybe even post to social media. In the middle of a crisis, people are going to need to be communicated with in several different ways. Things are going to be crazy and some people might not be able to receive phone calls but can get texts or emails. Others will be able to check social media. You will need to have a system that can do all of this or at least most of it. If you do use a system where you mainly use text, then ask about their capabilities of doing everything else in the middle of a crisis.

5. A system that can handle large call volumes and has a proven track record of doing that. Companies might be able to make calls, but you will need to make sure they can handle the volume you need. A situation like an ice storm, blizzard, tornado, or other event is not the time to find out your system won't work.

Off-site Website Access

If you'll notice, there are a lot of questions that we ask. It's not because I like talking to myself (even though most PR people do). It's mainly because we were asking ourselves these questions in the middle of the crisis. So, here is another one. If you lost your school servers, could you communicate through your school website? Some of you will answer "no." Some of you will answer, "I'm not sure." This is something important.

The minimum requirement that you need is the ability to log in and change the home page from any location or have someone that can do this with a quick phone call. Many organizations have an emergency page that replaces their website, and this gives you a place to display needed information and announcements. This is a must for any organization. You cannot have a stagnant home page or website in an emergency.

My personal preference would be to have a website that is hosted completely out of the district or at least off school property in a secure server that is not likely to be damaged in a local emergency like a tornado or fire or be offline in a winter storm. You can still have a locally designed and maintained website, but just make sure that you have it hosted outside of the area. You can also look at website companies that design and host your website for you.

If you do not have the ability to change your home page easily, place a link on your home page that is for emergency information. Then make sure that page is something you can access and change if the rest of your website cannot be accessed.

Social Media

There has been a lot of controversy over social media in schools, and in my opinion, a lot of it is unnecessary and is an overreaction. If you are not going to have social media for daily or regular communication in your school district, you need to have social media for use in an emergency. In many recent crisis situations, social media has been a major tool to communicate information and receive information. The Boston Police Department used it in the bombing to distribute facts.

In Joplin, the website was down, cell phone towers were gone, and phone lines were jammed. So, the district relied heavily on social media. When we were searching for the status of students and staff, the district asked people to post their status on the district Facebook page. The tornado caused people to be displaced, and many people left town to stay with relatives, friends, or even in hotels in area towns. This caused a problem in contacting people. So Facebook was one of the main methods of communication for the first several days of the crisis. When we were trying to contact 7,700 students and over 1,000 staff members with four phone lines, social media became a lifesaver.

Social media was also a great way to get messages and needs out for people to pass along. People were wanting to know what to do, what the district needed, what the status of the district was, if school was closed, what the summer school plans were, what students could do to get their stuff, and what statements were true and what were rumors.

A lot of these things were going around on social media anyway, so we needed to communicate on social media as well to be a part of the conversation and hopefully help to reduce rumors and communicate truth.

So, no matter what you do, I would have an emergency social media account for the district if you do not want to have one for the district to use regularly. It will be harder to get your message out if you do not already have followers on these, but it will be better than having nothing.

Get A Hotline

After going through the experience of Joplin and having to communicate out to people, going "old school" and having a hotline for people will now be a part of my communication and crisis plan. Things like a Google voice account are a great idea. It is off-site and can be used wherever you are. But, just having a hotline where you can record a message for students, parents, and staff will be a great tool. This can be used in minor crisis situations like snow days or severe weather.

Sometimes rapid notification systems cut out because of cell phone reception. So, having a hotline where you can upload a message that was the same district message that went out using your rapid notification system and other communication mediums will help reduce confusion. You can also look to do this for athletics and other events so there is one place for information. If you work to develop this system before a crisis, it will be the place people turn for information in a crisis because that is what they are used to doing.

The hotline system will allow you to communicate out messages to parents, students, and staff in a crisis situation. You may also want a separate "staff" hotline for that very reason. Staff communication was one area (which will be addressed later) that we struggled with at the beginning of the Joplin crisis, and it is something that you need to

A worker answers and makes phone calls on Monday, May 23, 2011, from Joplin North Middle School.

make sure is addressed early.

Frontline Staff

Those people answering your phones and interacting in the front office(s) during a crisis are some of the most important people you will have and will be working with in a crisis. They will be fielding calls and relaying information more than anyone else in the first few hours, so it is important to keep them informed.

You will want to develop talking points and fact sheets for things you know and things they can and cannot say and the correct answers to some of the questions that you know are going to come. Then update those things as needed and as they change, because they more than likely will.

You'll want to have some of those talking points already printed up or ready to be printed before a crisis happens. They would be things that you know are true and won't change. They are things like where to make monetary donations, where you will be posting information (those predetermined areas that shouldn't change), and a list of emergency numbers to places like the Red Cross and other relief organizations. Have discussions with the relief organizations before you print their numbers so you know that you are printing the correct ones for crisis situations.

You will also want to have forms ready that will be used in the first few hours of a crisis. The NSPRA manual has several of these forms that you can just copy, but there are also going to be district-specific forms that you will need (student information, hotline numbers, media requests, etc.). Ask what will be needed in a crisis and develop a packet for your frontline staff that can be easily copied and put into use. Your office managers know what questions they get all the time, so they will also have an idea of what they think will be the questions people are going to want to know.

Take time to train the staff members that will more than likely be your frontline people in a crisis. Doing this before the crisis happens is an important step. Just like the students need to practice to duck and cover or evacuating a building, your staff needs to practice what they need to do in a crisis situation.

Staff Communication Tools

In the middle of a crisis you cannot forget about your staff, but they will be the easiest ones to forget. This is not an intentional thing, but as you are faced with media, parents, major decisions, lawyers, etc., you will need to make sure you are communicating effectively with your staff.

The channel or method you will use to communicate is something you need to decide and communicate before a crisis. Put it in writing with a checklist so that you do not forget what you are supposed to do or about the groups with which you need to communicate. This is where that hotline would come into play along with an intranet, phone calls, text messages, websites, etc.

In a crisis, communicate in the predetermined ways and then also be open to communicating in other necessary ways. You might not be able to use phone communication, so you might have to rely more on one method over the other. It is always a good idea to post the messages in multiple places.

I have started texting our administration information when events happen so they hear it first. There are several group texting apps or systems that you can use so you only have to send the information out once to several people.

During the crisis, you may need to plan regular meetings/gatherings for staff to obtain information. They will want to meet with their administrator, and may also want to meet with the superintendent. The superintendent will need to make sure that he/she does a good job at meeting with staff while balancing the other 100 things that are occurring. The staff will want to hear from their leader. And, in the case where communication is spotty because of the lack of phones and Internet, the in-person meetings can be very beneficial.

Diagrams and Visuals

You are going to be dealing with all types of people. Visual aids are some of the most powerful things that you can have in a crisis. People

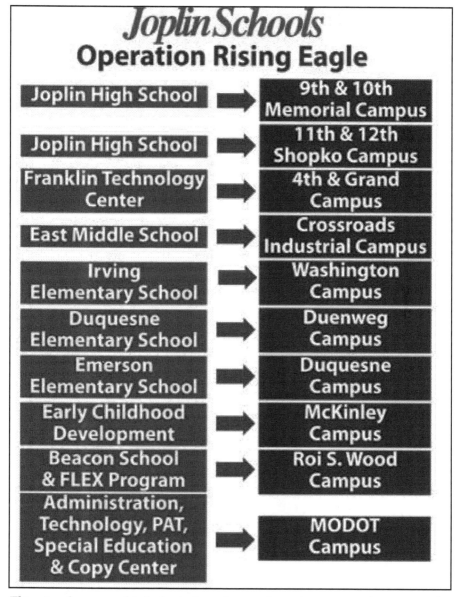

This visual was used to help students know where they were going to attend school in the fall of 2011.

want a face to put with the crisis to help them identify with it in a personal way. They also want a picture to help them understand what is going on.

So, when possible, use diagrams, and visuals (photos, backdrops, etc.) to help expand on what you are saying. For example, when Joplin made the decision to combine schools, move schools, and find new locations for the next school year, they used a diagram. This was something simple that people could refer to so they could find where they were going to school.

One of the most touching moments that I remember was when Dr. Huff read a letter from a child who had sent in one dollar because she wanted to help. He held up the letter at a press conference to show how much people were helping from across the nation.

You can also use things like charts and graphs to show percentages, maps to show locations, or any other aid to help communicate your message effectively.

Plan For Dignitaries:

In the days, weeks, months, and years after the tornado, it was not an

Missouri Commissioner of Education Chris Nicastro was one of the first Missouri officials to visit Joplin Schools after the tornado struck. Here she meets with Dr. CJ Huff, Joplin superintendent, at the Joplin High School campus just days after the tornado struck.

Missouri Governor Jay Nixon was a consistent presence in Joplin in the days and weeks after the tornado. Here he holds a press conference at Missouri Southern State University, which was a staging ground for many aspects of the tornado recovery efforts.

uncommon occurrence in Joplin to have some State or Federal official visiting. Because of the security measures that have to be taken when these people visit, you will need to designate a staff member for this job since preparing for visits can be a long-term process and/or take several man-hours to prepare for the visit with the advance team and assistants who will need very specific requests met. It will also speed up the process if someone learns the "in's and out's" of visits. Not every event will call for this, but having a person who has this as his or her job in the crisis plan will help since people will know who the person in charge of those visits will be.

Plan For Community or Student Gatherings:

Whether you want to be a part of an event or not, the district will get pulled into situations that will be outside of what you want anything to do with.

One of those was when the students at Joplin High School wanted to all get together. This was during a time when emotions were high and the Westboro Baptist Church members were coming into town. The students were planning on meeting at the local Target parking lot. Think about an event where a couple of thousand students wanted to gather and the possibility of media and the Westboro Baptist Church there. Sounds fun, huh? The students then wanted to move the event to Jung Stadium. Now we have students coming onto school property so it would be a school event and involve a whole other list of things. The event went back and forth between Target and Jung a few times, and I got to know the safety coordinator for Target quite well. Thankfully, a local church stepped in and wanted to host the event after hearing of it from a few students. They rented the stadium and made it a private event where they asked that all media and non-students were to be kept out. This helped out the situation, but emotions were still raw at this point in time and we had no clue how all this would go.

As Curtis and I were pulling into the stadium just to be there in case they needed a school official, a massive lightning storm came into the city and the event was canceled. I've never been more thankful for lightning in my life. With all of the craziness of the day and the event, I don't think the city could have handled any drama that might have come from the event with all of the external factors involved.

Outside of this situation, the school might have the largest gathering space in your community, so it might become the natural spot for people to gather. So, make sure you know your district's policies on gatherings, memorials, demonstrations, and any other event that would fall in this list or make sure you develop them if you don't have them. Is the event public or private based on the situation and what role does the district play in each? Having this known now will help when a situation like this comes up in your district. In addition, make contact with those who have large gathering areas in your community. This might be Wal-Mart, Target, your city park, or a place of worship, but having contact information for their security people will help prevent you from having to call the store operator when you need them.

PART 2: PREPARE

Notes:

CHAPTER 9: PLAN AHEAD

Complacency is our worst enemy. We think nothing bad could happen, "we are completely prepared," or "we have time to prepare and things can wait." Other things get in our way, and we lose focus or a sense of importance if we aren't directly dealing with something. Just look at how schools reacted after things like Columbine or how the nation reacted after September 11. After a while, the importance fades, and we get back to the daily grind. Our focus is always on "what is at hand" and "what is unknown" is just on a list of "to-do" things on our desk. We think we can wait until another day to do it, but in reality, that day never really comes.

Then, the unknown or unexpected happens, and we wish we had taken a few extra moments to plan or just a couple more moments to train. There is a reason why we have fire drills, tornado drills, earthquake drills, and intruder drills. They keep us focused and remind us what is important. But how often do we plan outside of the "duck and cover" and evacuation? We tend to never ask those important questions, so we never get answers or solutions. We go through these drills but never take the planning further.

I hope you never have to go through something catastrophic, but we still need to plan for even the most basic crisis. Then, we will be able to act and react in the most effective way possible.

We've all been told about the waves in things in a crisis, but those also come months and years after. Joplin is still riding waves of different events and will be for years into the future. As stated before, this comes with the first time something happens after the crisis (first day of school, first dance, next graduation, etc.). However, there are things that can cause more ripples like construction issues, elections, rumors, and others events that you will not even dream of planning for.

When events happen it changes your school and community, and you will deal with the ripples for an extensive period of time, sometimes decades into the future. Find a school district or community that had a major crisis event, and you will more than likely find a community that is still dealing with some aspect of the event from years in the past.

However, in the middle of a crisis event or anything going on in your school or community, you can't forget to stop and think and breathe. Not everything is a checklist. People are involved, and they will be dealing with their emotions (both good and bad) during a crisis. Sometimes it is okay to just stop and celebrate or grieve or decompress and then get back at what you were doing.

This is why the planning process is so important. You can work out details and develop a structure for your school district to react to what is thrown at it. If you can work to plan for the structure and practice that, you can translate those basic elements into multiple crisis situations.

CHAPTER 10:
WHY DO YOU NEED A
COMMUNICATION PROGRAM?

by Dr. Stephen Kleinsmith, superintendent of Nixa Public Schools

Communicating effectively is the number one "leadership" characteristic needed by superintendents. That's not to suggest that other characteristics are less important, but excellent communication skills are a prerequisite for the others to emerge. For example, how can a superintendent demonstrate being a visionary goal-achiever without effectively communicating the vision and goals? How can one be a champion team-builder without effectively communicating with the team? Or, how can one be a progressive change-agent without effectively communicating the process needed to bring about those changes? Without communication, understanding is impossible, conflicts are probable, and educational progress is limited.

This prerequisite skill called "communication" is everlasting... it will never be outdated, only improved upon. If we believe that the educational change process is constant and ongoing, then the school's communication process must also be constant and ongoing. Superintendents must not only have excellent communication skills themselves, but they must emphasize the importance of effective communications by making it the responsibility of everyone in the school system, and never forgetting that good PR begins in the classroom.

Parents often judge the school district based on what they hear from

Dr. Kleinsmith addresses members of the Nixa Public Schools' staff as well as Nixa community members during a strategic planning meeting.

their children, the teachers and what they hear from other parents. Therefore, it is critical that the vision, values, and direction of the superintendent are clearly communicated to all staff, in messages that are easily understood, aligned with, and repeated in as many settings as possible (verbal, print, media, etc.). If a child says something at home about the school, the parents often assume that the child has spoken for the teacher, the principal, or the superintendent. It takes hard work and time for the parents to investigate and evaluate whether the child's statements are based on the reality of the situation or the intent of the superintendent who is responsible for everything that happens in that classroom.

One way to emphasize the importance of effective communication is to role model such behavior in as many daily routines as possible in providing leadership throughout the district and the community at large. Experience and best practices have taught most superintendents the value and importance of clear, open communications. As a communicator, the superintendent must be able to write clearly, listen effectively, and speak articulately and avoid educational jargon. After all, writing and speaking are basic skills being taught to our students, and the superintendent must proficiently demonstrate those skills.

Excellent superintendents have a high level of interaction with others and communicate with people in a manner that builds positive, harmonious relations. That's why it so important to "get out of the office" often, even wearing tennis shoes if necessary, in order to just get out among the people who are being served. That's why so many superintendents are "seen" and heard from during events open to the public. Sporting events, chamber meetings, ministerial alliance gatherings, PTA functions, and student assemblies are but a few examples found on the superintendent's weekly calendar of events. Simply put, visibility is a part of communication and being visible reinforces the public's understanding of the superintendent's role. By doing so, an important by-product is the enjoyment of sharing the positive things happening within the schools, interacting with colleagues and patrons alike, and most important, "listening one's way to solutions!"

Communication is particularly important to superintendents because they are responsible to such a varied and large list of constituents. As they say, superintendents walk with elephants' feet and wear many hats in doing so. The position and duties of the superintendent are important, especially to the community being served, and that importance must be acknowledged. District leaders usually have a well-developed ability to transmit ideas, thoughts, and programs. They have a powerful set of beliefs and can use them effectively. When people read or hear about the superintendent, they are automatically considering this the voice of the expert. This is not for personal gain, nor should it be. Rather it is to obtain and maintain leadership of the public's opinion and perception of the district in a way that best benefits the students.

Abraham Lincoln expressed this philosophy best over 150 years ago when he said, "Public sentiment is everything – with it, nothing can fail; without it, nothing can succeed." So, it would be wise for any superintendent to remember this before proposing the implementation of a new idea (i.e. magnet school) or passing another bond issue or levy increase. The "willingness to risk" is less risky for the superintendent who has developed a strong impression, or reputation, as an expert in the field. When there is a large base of followers who obviously trust and believe in the superintendent's vision of the future and mission of the district, then most proposals that are clearly seen as good for the students will readily gain approval. If this kind of trust and support (all built on a foundation of effective communication) is not present, then the job becomes one of putting out fires. Firefighters are paid to be reactive; superintendents are paid to be proactive, and will likely not be retained by the school board if they consistently operate in the reaction zone.

Communication is not just talking. As stated earlier, listening one's way to solutions can be a very effective way of building up public sentiment and for gaining much needed support for ideas wished to be embraced by the community. A well-developed and comprehensive communication program is not just a laundry list of nice activities to make everyone "feel" good about the district. PR is not a smoke screen or a cover up for problems. Nor is it a remedy or an attempt to get everyone in agreement on every issue. Rather, an effective communication strategy requires the practice of positive PR (i.e. good relationships) with individuals and groups who interact with the schools, students, staff, parents, taxpayers, legislators, and others in the community in order for them to believe in what the district is doing and not just "feel" good about it.

For superintendents, developing a communication program is not only a foundation for leadership, it is a critical responsibility based on the legal and moral obligation to listen to the public and to keep them informed. To do this, there are a few basic elements of external and internal communications to consider:

EXAMPLES OF EXTERNAL COMMUNICATION ELEMENTS

- DISTRICT WEBSITE – This should be the central hub of information for the district. Since most people looking for information on the district will do an online search, having an updated, appealing, and, most of all, easily navigable website should be a district's top priority.

- COMMUNITY NEWSLETTER – This should be issued on a regular basis and distributed to all households in the district, not just parents of children in the public schools. Some districts regularly send e-newsletters to their parents or community. If it is a community newsletter, it should be an opt-in e-newsletter so the district isn't accused of spamming recipients. However, depending on your community, not all people have email and the district won't have access to email addresses of non-parents. Therefore, a printed newsletter may be an option to keep members of your community informed. This is where knowing your community is important so you can effectively reach them in the best way.

- NEWS MEDIA RELATIONS – This should be an organized program to provide news releases and story ideas about the district to radio, television, online, and print media. This district should establish guidelines as to whom the media should contact either for that story or for all media inquiries. The district should also reach out to be a resource to help explain various topics like school finance or curriculum even when the story isn't about the district.

- COMMUNITY & BUSINESS EVENTS – Attending these events is another technique for familiarizing community leaders and non-

Zac Rantz and Dr. Stephen Kleinsmith participate in the Nixa Chamber of Commerce's "Ugly Christmas Sweater" contest. Nixa Chamber Director Marc Truby announces that Dr. Kleinsmith is the winner of the contest.

parents with their schools and their programs, and in turn, demonstrating to the community that the district also supports their local businesses and community organizations and events.

- OpEd ARTICLES - Newspapers often look to educational leaders in the community for their opinions on local, state, and national educational issues. This is not a soapbox, but rather it is a great opportunity to provide a well-thought-out analysis of an issue and support it with examples that are relevant to the community.

- OPINION SURVEYS – Two-way communication is the key to success, and while getting into the community to find out what people are thinking is good, formally soliciting feedback in surveys can bring about an even better understanding of what the broader community is thinking and not just anecdotal information from one citizen here or there. Survey results can also be used as formal data when researching various issues.

- PROGRAM BROCHURES – Special education, psychological services, kindergarten, the lunch program, Title I, etc., can be explained in brochures which are distributed to staff, parents, and community members or made available at various points of entry into the community (City Hall, Chamber of Commerce, realtor offices, etc.).

- COMMUNITY/ADULT EDUCATION PROGRAMS – Seventy percent of the households in America do not have public school-aged youngsters. Therefore, these kinds of programs can be an important vehicle for bringing the general public inside the schools. Partnering with a local university or technical college can also expand the district's offerings.

- SPEAKERS' BUREAU – This is a pre-identified group of administrators, board members, and teachers who have excellent verbal communication skills and are available to address community and parent groups on topics related to education and the school system.

Developing talking points and consistent presentations will help ensure that the message being distributed is consistent and will help the message "stick" in the community.

- WELCOME KIT – A package of information about the district, especially statistics about student enrollment and achievement, should be distributed to new residents through the Chamber of Commerce, city, Welcome Wagon, local banks, and others. People have made, what is more than likely, a long-term investment in a house, and they need to feel reassured that their purchase in the community was a correct one.

- DISCOUNT PROGRAM FOR SENIOR CITIZENS – As taxpayers, seniors often feel they don't get any tangible return on their dollar, so why not issue them "Gold Card" passes, along with annual activity schedules, which allow them free or reduced admittance to programs such as athletics, music, and drama?

- CITIZEN ADVISORY COMMITTEES – These committees can study and supply valuable input on items such as textbooks, curriculum, bond and levy elections, building programs, and many other items which affect the local school system and which are paid for by their tax dollars.

EXAMPLES OF INTERNAL COMMUNICATION ELEMENTS

Internal communication should be a primary focus when building or rebuilding trust in the community. The work a district puts in to a campaign or initiative can be undone if the district does not have effective internal communication.

- STAFF NEWSLETTER – These should be distributed on a regular basis to ALL employees: certified and support, full and part-time (including substitute staff). Districts could also send a newsletter to retired district employees to keep them connected to the district. Making this a required method of communication for staff to read

As a part of Nixa's new teacher orientation program, new staff to Nixa have a lunch provided by the Nixa Chamber of Commerce where new Nixa teachers are able to be introduced to local community members and elected officials.

will help make sure important updates are seen. Districts can also explore making this newsletter an e-newsletter to reduce paper clutter and give staff one place to receive important district information.

- BOARD MEETING HIGHLIGHTS – This should be issued the morning after each board meeting and distributed to staff and community leaders, as well as the media. Routinely distributing it ensures that the staff and public get continual messages and not just when there is a "hot" issue brewing.

- STAFF HANDBOOKS – These are district-level handbooks for certified and support staff, with a summary of important policies, procedures, and general information applicable to each group, as well as names, titles, phone numbers, and email addresses for administrative staff.

- NEW EMPLOYEE ORIENTATION – There should be as least one of these at the beginning of each year; more often if the school system is large and has new employees joining the staff throughout the year. Starting all staff off on the right foot with the same consistent information will help ensure their success in the district.

- SUPERINTENDENT'S CABINET – This is an advisory group to the superintendent that meets on a regular basis to keep the boss up-to-date on what's happening in the field and "prompting" attention and/or attendance of the superintendent at events and happenings that might not otherwise have been reported or on the schedule. This also allows various topics to be discussed from various viewpoints before decisions are made.

- ADMINISTRATION/STAFF/BOARD STUDY COMMITTEES – These provide an opportunity for tangible staff involvement in issues affecting a myriad of school issues. As staff feel like they have the ability to voice their opinions on various issues, they will gain more ownership in the district.

- STAFF RECOGNITION AND AWARDS PROGRAMS – It is important that these are organized programs that not only provide a needed "pat on the back" for a job well-done, but focuses the attention of the entire staff to tangible achievements that were genuinely needed and sincerely appreciated in the district. It is nice to recognize years of service and retirements, but they should also be tied to the achievements of the individual whenever possible. Also consider a way for staff to recognize each other so it is not just the principal or superintendent recognizing staff.

- IN-SERVICE FOR CERTIFIED AND SUPPORT STAFF – These programs should include full and part-time employees, teachers, secretaries, bus drivers, cafeteria staff, administrators, etc. – everyone in the "school family" in order to train them in their roles as school communicators. Districts work to equip them in other areas but many times do not provide ways for staff to improve their communication skills even though they serve as the district's ambassadors in the community.

- STAFF SURVEYS – Communication can't be all one-way, so it is necessary to occasionally survey the staff to solicit their input and opinions on key issues. Be careful not to over survey your staff or they will become indifferent. Also, only ask if you plan on using the data. Staff will also become indifferent if they do not feel their participation has any benefit.

- STUDENT ADVISORY COUNCIL – This group can be particularly valuable at the secondary level, so students can be involved in providing input on issues and activities in the district. Many times they see things from a different perspective and can offer valuable information to the district.

- COMMUNICATIONS COMPONENT IN ALL MAJOR PROGRAMS – Whether it's a renewed stress on basic skills, a program to eradicate vandalism, or a plan to improve discipline in the schools, every major project undertaken by a school district should begin at the planning stages with a "charter" that delineates a written communications component that specifies how and when the goals, objectives, and activities will be disseminated to both the internal and external publics.

Because superintendents have many assignments, an effective communication program is often placed on the "nice-to-do" list and doesn't get serious consideration as a necessary programmatic approach district-wide. However, the superintendent with the highest leadership scores will be the one who starts with a comprehensive communication strategy and who truly understands that it is the necessary prerequisite to effectively use the rest of their leadership skills. And, while it may be difficult to justify, having a communication professional in the district to oversee and champion these efforts will repay the district multiple times over. Many superintendents say they didn't know they needed a communication professional until they had one, and, now that they do, they will never be without one.

CHAPTER 11:
COMMUNICATION AND COMMUNITY OUTREACH

If you ask Dr. Huff why they were able to recover so quickly and have the network of help that developed, he will credit the community relations and communication program they had established prior to the tornado striking. FEMA even made the comment that the community effort was unusual and the outreach they had done prior to the tornado was the foundation to their success.

They made a conscious effort to reach out to their community and develop lines of communication and also develop programs to help meet the needs of their students. They worked to build relationships and engagement. They even won a national award for their Bright Futures program, which is designed as a way the community can help meet the needs of the students in Joplin.

Why is all of this important to you? Well, this is why you need a communication professional or at least some form of an organized communications and community outreach program in your district. As C. Northcote Parkinson said, "The void created by the failure to communicate is soon filled with poison, drivel, and misrepresentation." You can either have others make up their own story about your district, or you can show them the truth about your district and bring them in to be a part of it.

Members of Nixa's Safety and Security Team hold up free school lunch passes donated by OPAA! Food Management that were handed out to local first responders and law enforcement members as a way to help increase the presence of safety officials in schools as well as a way to say "thank you" for all the work they do.

I've heard superintendents say that you don't know you need a communication professional until you have one (as Dr. Kleinsmith referenced in the previous chapter), and then you don't know what you'd do without one. Having someone who has a communication background or whom you designate and train to be the communication professional is something that districts need. I know that in many districts this is the superintendent, but you need someone who specializes or has specific training in communications and public relations if at all possible. There is a science to and a reason behind what is and is not done and said, and you need someone on your staff with that knowledge.

The old way of communicating won't work. The idea that you don't talk to the media or say "no comment" or don't engage your public is gone. We live in a 24-hour world. We live in a society that expects two-way communication. We have had to adapt how we educate our students to meet them where they are. We have to do the same with communication in our schools. You will need to embrace new technologies and communicate with people in the way that they want to be communicated to and with. It might take you out of your comfort zone, but schools have to stop thinking like they are islands. We are not. We are one part of a community, and we can either engage that community and find success or disengage and wonder why support for our district isn't there.

Nixa has a very successful communication program. We strive to engage our community. We are a part of them and they are a part of us. It isn't an "us vs. them" mentality. It is common to see the Chamber of Commerce, city officials, and county officials all working together with the school, and the school working with them. You need the same community engagement in your district. For some of you it will be hard, but the investment is worth the payoff. Seek out people to help you. Get people involved. Build trust in the schools. You have to tell the good, the bad, and the ugly to gain trust. If there are problems in your schools, show people how they can help take the "frog" and make it a "prince."

Joplin did that. Before the tornado, they showed how over 54% of their families live in poverty. Then they showed how people could help make that situation better for those students. They built up the network of support. They built partnerships and trust. They started the Bright Futures program. Then, at the hour of their greatest need, those people stepped in and showed what can be done when a community works together.

We all thought that Dr. Huff was a little crazy when he wanted to start school in less than 90 days after the tornado damaged or destroyed half of Joplin and damaged or destroyed half of the buildings in the school district. But, he knew what the community was capable of, and he saw a network that was just waiting to react and help. They did it. In less than 90 days students were back in the classroom. It gave their students and staff a safe place to go and a sense of normalcy in a still chaotic situation. Together the school district and community created a common cause and moved heaven and earth to accomplish something amazing.

The public has a perception of your district or schools. It might not be an accurate perception, but it is a perception and that is what you have to deal with. You have to work to move them to what "reality" is, but you have to meet them where they are and then show them what is true and what is false. Over time, they will develop a sense of trust in your district, and their perception will turn into a clearer reflection of reality.

You don't want the only time that people hear about your school in the media to be when something bad happens. If that's all they hear, then that will be what they think is true. So, you also need an effective media relations program. Media professionals have deadlines. They need to be in and out as soon as possible with a story. If you cause them problems, they aren't going to cover news in your district because it just isn't worth their time. They can't waste their whole day dealing with your red tape. The good reporters actually want to give a balanced look at a school district, but they can't do that if you don't or won't let them. Work with them and ask them what they need for a story. They just want someone to tell the story and give them the facts so they can report it. It's not that hard.

When we needed the media to help communicate important information about Joplin Schools, I was able to contact the media professionals who I work so closely with as communications director at Nixa Public Schools, and they helped. We can't forget that we are all in this together. With all of the craziness in Joplin, they were one of the major forces getting information out in the region.

I firmly believe a communications program is no longer an extra thing or a luxury in a district. It has to be ingrained in every aspect of the district. Districts must listen to their community, and they must create a two-way communication system. The business community has seen the need for an effective public relations program for many years.

Why aren't schools seeing the same thing? It paid off for Joplin. Make sure you have a system in place so that when you need your community to help, the network is already established.

Learn To Work With Your Local Government Groups

As you are planning ahead, don't forget to plan outside of your school or organization. You are not a lone island that will not have to interact with anyone else in a crisis. You have to work to plan with your local government and relief groups now.

Developing effective lines of communication now with your local government will help prevent some of the fighting and frustration that occurs in every crisis. You are going to be spending a lot of time interacting with each other in a major crisis. So, go ahead and accept the fact that you are going to make someone mad; you both just deal with it and move on. Emotions are high and people will be tired, and, at some point in time, you are going to want to slap the person next to you. But, this has to stay within the organization or your small group. If you have built those lines of communication and a sense of trust between local groups, you'll be able to work through these moments of high emotion.

One of the most important things to remember is that in the middle of a crisis, people don't really care if you like each other or not, they just want you to solve the problem. If you are an elected official or official in the community, while you might not be directly involved or in charge of a situation, it is your issue whether you like it or not. So, you have to learn to play nice or at least learn to fake playing nice.

Break down the barriers now and get to know each other. You have to be able to work together in everyday situations so that when a crisis happens, you have a foundation to build upon.

One of the best relationships for the communication professional in your district to have is with the public information officers (or the person who will function in that position) for the city and county. Your bosses might not be talking, but you need to have open lines of communication. If you can build from there and eventually have regular meetings with the city, county, and school, you will reap the rewards when a crisis happens.

Above all, your community needs to see and show that you can lead together. When people's lives and livelihoods are on the line, their government and community entities need to work together. This has to be developed prior to any sort of crisis.

The Piggy Bank Philosophy

To help illustrate why you need successful communication and community outreach, think of a piggy bank. What you put into the piggy bank is what you can withdraw from the piggy bank.

So, I work to fill my school's piggy bank with positive news stories and stories and photos of things that they might not know about if we don't actively let the community know about it. These are my deposits. This helps build the community's perception of the school district.

Now, you may not think that you have much to promote, but you do. You have stories of test scores that went up. Maybe it wasn't as high as you wanted, but you are making progress. Also, don't forget to tell the stories of your students and staff. Find those unique stories and help tell them. If the media won't cover it, find a way to get it out on your website or newsletters. If you always realize there is a story to tell, you will always be on the look out for it.

stock.xchng image

As you keep making these deposits, you then have something to withdraw from when (not if, but when) something negative happens in your school district. It could be something small or it could be a big scandal. But, if you have worked to fill your piggy bank with stories that build trust and a good perception in the school district, you will have something you can withdraw from. You may spend it all, but at least your "perception debt" won't be as low as it could have been.

If you haven't worked to fill your piggy bank with anything, then you are fully in the debt of what the news media reports and what public perception becomes. And, the hole you have to dig yourself out of will be much deeper and take much longer than if you had put the work in before.

I have seen many school districts go through this and the perception they had in the past is still around 20 to 30 years later because they did not work to make positive deposits and their reputation of one negative event still lingers.

CHAPTER 12:
REVIEW POLICIES AND PROCEDURES

Board/District Policies

You will want to review your board policies and see what situations they cover. This review should be an annual procedure for your district. In Joplin, we were in the middle of some situations and were looking through Joplin's board policies and realized that some hadn't been updated since the late 1980's or early 1990's. They were in the middle of a switch to the Missouri School Boards' Association's policy system, but some things had changed since their old policies were written. There were regular and emergency board meetings to approve new policies. I called back to my district several times that first week just asking if we had certain policies in place. I don't think schools or businesses realize how important policies or business plans are until you need them, then you sometimes feel like you are scrambling to find them. So, review all of those policies and make sure they are up-to-date. You need to make sure that your board policies address at least the following:

1.   emergency purchasing

2.   emergency building repairs

3.   media/public interaction policies

4.   securing your district

5.   securing district property

6.   emergency hiring

7.   student information and FERPA

Your district will need to be able to buy things, make emergency decisions, and control who is on your property during a crisis. So, having those plans and policies in place now will give your district and leadership team the authority to do what needs to be done in the middle of a crisis.

This is also a good time for me to plug having a policy service through an organization or having some sort of organization that reviews laws and can help you by developing policies for your organization.

The Three-Month Reserve

Your business office is going to be one of the most important offices at the beginning of and for the remainder of a crisis. Getting a district back up and running and able to pay people and make purchases will be critical.

In order to do this, you will need to be able to have cash on hand to make purchases. Dr. Huff has stated that having a three-month reserve saved the district at the beginning until cash donations really started flowing in. It will be the same for your district. Do you have enough money in reserves to operate for three months if needed?

In tough economic times when states are cutting funding for schools, having a three-month reserve will also help if the money just doesn't come in on time or they withhold funds at the last minute. That right there is a crisis in and of itself.

It might not be your practice as a district now, but this is a practice that your district should really consider implementing to help prepare for a crisis (either economic, natural, or some other kind).

The Accounting Nightmare

At the beginning of the crisis in Joplin, things just needed to be purchased and done, but looking back on the situation, taking time to set up different accounting procedures early would have helped in the tracking of money and purchases.

When you are dealing with FEMA or your insurance, you have to report what you are spending money on. What would work best is if you can designate certain funds and codes to be used for crisis purchasing or emergency situations. That way, you already have those in place if something happens and you can refer back to those codes and funds instead of having to try to figure out what you were spending for the situation and what was normal district expenditures. You'll have to separate it all out, so take some time and do that now and then make sure and place all of those codes and procedures in your crisis plan.

The Donation Nightmare

At the beginning of any crisis, one of the main things people want to know is how they can help. People will start bringing in things just to do something. So, you need to have a plan.

Joplin Schools started receiving bags of stuff (very random stuff like old clothes or used furniture) right after the tornado hit. Now I know that people wanted something to do to help, and this was their way of doing that. But, districts and organizations need to be prepared for what they want and do not want to do with donations.

People also just kept bringing in things, like water. Lots and lots of water. There was water on street corners, in parking lots, and everywhere else you looked, and it just kept coming. People thought that was what was needed, so they just kept bringing it.

In order to prevent people from just bringing what they think you need,

In the weeks and months that followed the tornado, Joplin Schools received many various kinds of donations that included school supplies as well as personal hygiene items and clothing. It took them almost six months to go through all of the donations. Once they moved into their temporary central office space, a distribution center (pictured above) was developed to help keep a record of what had been donated as well as have an efficient way to distribute the supplies to the students who needed them.

I recommend the following:

- Do not accept product donations until you know what you need and what you want to do with them. Otherwise, you are just going to have to do something with the products and materials that people bring.

- Do accept monetary donations. You are going to need some money at the beginning to get things you need. You are also going to need money to make some projects happen, so this is going to be both a short and long-term solution.

- Do set up emergency bank accounts now. The middle of a crisis is not when you want to figure out where monetary donations need to go, and, since there is paperwork involved, that will not be something you want to deal with then. Get these set up now. You will want to also encourage any education foundations or similar organizations to do the same. By having a system in place for donations, you can direct people effectively at the beginning of a crisis. Some districts might choose to have an account within their current accounting structure for donations. Either way, review what is the best for your district so you have it set up now.

- Do set up a way to take credit cards now. You may not be able to handle credit card processing through your normal business office at this point in time, but having it set up for emergencies where you can put a "Donate" button on your website in a matter of minutes will be a major plus in the middle of the chaos. You can tell people you need money and give them a link to donate.

- Do get your donation process in writing and include it in your crisis plan. This should be a piece of paper that can be copied and distributed easily to the public. It should also be something that you give to those answering phones in the district or organization. There were offers for donations coming in early and a few big ones got sent to the wrong place because the process wasn't in the hands of the ones answering the phones. There is nothing like sending one million dollars to the wrong place for you to get your processes lined out really quickly.

- Do not become a distribution center if you can prevent it. In some communities, this isn't an option, but there will be distribution centers popping up all over the place and some major organizations like the Red Cross or Convoy of Hope will have things set up fairly quickly. This is one more thing that you don't want to have to deal with. You should let the people who do this professionally do it. They are the experts. Don't try to reinvent the wheel. One of your buildings might have to serve as a location because of the nature of the event, but not being in charge of this, if at all possible, is an important thing.

- Do inform people early and often what the donation plan is both before a crisis hits and also during a crisis. In an emergency, people might not hear or actually listen to the message the first time. Repeating it, posting it, and printing it out will need to happen.

- Do designate a donation coordinator now. This person should work to get everything set-up and have a plan of action for what will occur in the event of a crisis. Don't forget to have a backup person, and, of course, get the plans in writing and secured in an off-site location. (Do you notice a theme developing?) And, make sure you have all donation calls going through this one office.

- Do learn that saying "Thank you, but no" or "Thank you, but not right now" is okay. It may be a great offer, but if it isn't going to help for that situation, you have to do what is right for the district.

- Do learn to reach out to people to help. It could be a phone call or just a list of needs that is updated daily online. Dish Network sent a team to set up TVs and satellite dishes so we could actually get news and see what was going on. Davis Cellular and Verizon were quick to help us get MiFi hotspots because we asked them to help meet a need.

One unintended consequence of promoting the donations that were coming in was that the public thought that Joplin Schools received more money than what they really did. The district made a huge deal with kids that brought in just a few dollars, and that was the right thing to do. They treated the business that brought in thousands of dollars the same as a child who collected a jar of coins. But just be aware of the perception you are creating. There was some confusion in Joplin when the district had to ask for a $60 million Bond Issue to help finish construction. Things like a visual diagram showing how much is left to raise to rebuild will help show that you are making progress yet are still short of your final goal and put in perspective what is going on as far as donations.

Insurance

The last thing you need to worry about in the middle of a crisis is what your insurance will or will not cover. You don't need to find out after

On the first day of school since the tornado, the entrance to the temporary Joplin High School for 11th and 12th grade students that was built in a empty store at Northpark Mall in Joplin lies quiet and empty.

something is destroyed that your insurance won't cover it.

Also, you need to ask not only if the building is covered but also any temporary structure until the permanent one is rebuilt. It took three years to rebuild Joplin High School. There were several additional expenses in the interim. One of the major expenses is the 11th and 12th grade center at the Joplin mall. The school district not only had to lease the space, but it had to be remodeled for students. This multi-million dollar investment is something that has to be paid for somehow. Knowing who pays for what now will help you plan for what could happen.

Check with your business department on what is covered in their part of the plan. People and businesses will need to be paid, and you will need a business office up and running as soon as possible. Does your insurance cover being set up immediately after a disaster? If not, I'd suggest looking into that. My district is making sure that we have a plan that covers the business office being up and running in some form 24-48 hours after a disaster that displaces the business office. These are things that need to be established with your core operating systems and departments as well.

Having an accurate and up-to-date list of the items in your buildings will come in handy when a disaster strikes. Years after the tornado hit, this is still something that Joplin brings up in the discussions. When a disaster takes the contents of your buildings and distributes them along a debris field several miles long, an inventory list (with photos and video if possible) stored off-site is a gold mine. You have to be able to prove what was in your buildings in order for it to be covered. Having the list on your computer or in your desk really won't do you much good when that computer is in a field two miles away or everything is ruined in a fire. Also, make sure that your staff keeps a list of what personal items they have in their classrooms or offices. They will need that for their claims and you'll need it to determine what is school property and what is personal property.

As good as your insurance may be, they will only pay you back for what you had, not what you need. So, if you only had materials for 1,500 students and your school held 2,000, you only get covered for the 1,500 number.

What Do You Do With Staff?

In the middle of the chaos of a crisis that incapacitates the school district or even just a building, on top of the major decisions you have to make, you will also have your faculty and staff members wondering what they are supposed to do.

While you might be tempted to just tell them to stay home, can you legally do that? Is that breaking their contract with the district? How does that impact their salaries? Will they be paid? Can they be paid without clocking in? Who has the power to make these decisions? Do your policies allow for these decisions to be made easily?

Those might not seem like major questions, but you need to have a plan. Have it in writing so that whoever has to execute this part of your crisis plan knows exactly what to tell people.

Your staff are going to want to help, so you need to have a volunteer plan. This will look different for your salary vs. hourly employees. Your hourly employees aren't on the same contract as your salaried employees, so you need to know if you are going to pay them without work for a certain amount of time and not require them to work. Or, are you going to require that they report to certain locations to help out as needed.

You also need to know what you are going to require of your contracted employees. Do they all have to work a certain amount? What about those that can't? Do they have to take personal days?

Whether staff work or volunteer, you need to ask yourself what you will do when there isn't any work to be done. Do you just want people sitting around? You might be thinking that in a crisis situation there will always be work to do, but there was downtime when we just had to wait. There were no more buildings to clean because half of them were damaged and mopping them would have been pretty pointless. The clerical staff can do a lot of processing of documents, but what about your paraprofessionals and similar positions. What do they do to earn their salaries?

Develop plans and even board policies as needed. Give people the authority they need in these situations to determine what needs to happen and how to handle contracts and pay checks. It's easier to have this discussion now than in the middle of a crisis.

One of the major lessons to learn is that if you don't have the right people in the right positions in your district now, a crisis event will exacerbate the issues. Learn that you need the right staff in the right positions now. This might require staffing changes, but it is better to move positions or make some changes now. We must do the right thing for our students, and they deserve the best we can give them.

CHAPTER 13: MOVE THINGS OFF-SITE

Contrary to popular belief, a flash drive that you take home with you each night is not considered an "off-site file backup." In the middle of a crisis that takes out your critical systems, having a backup off-site will be one of the best resources you have. Why? Well, you will need to access your student lists when you may have lost power. So, having a physical student list is good. If you have an online back up system, make sure you will be able to access it during a crisis.

You also want to backup and even have access to your most critical systems off-site or in a secure bunker. I would recommend off-site as the best option. In the case of Joplin, the administration center had a bunker, but it was without power, and they had to deal with water in the basement. They did get a generator to the systems, but if the tornado had taken a slightly more northern path, the systems would have been even more damaged and even more inaccessible.

To get the systems up and running, a crew had to wade through the water in the administration center's basement with head lamps to get the servers up and running so they could run payroll and access student data. It worked, but having those accessible from the command center would have been a much easier option.

So, to prepare, make sure critical systems have backups outside the district or in a secure bunker, at the very least. You also need to ask how the backup systems work and know what will happen if part of the backup system goes down. Will your information still be there because there is a redundant part of the backup? Good to know that now and not in the middle of a crisis.

If you have a secure bunker, can water get in? How about fire? Is there a backup generator to keep things running if needed? You need to make sure that your systems can still function or will be secure in a variety of situations. A system that is in a bunker but isn't functional is a waste of time and money.

If you cannot implement an off-site backup or a secure bunker, keep your main or important servers off the upper floors in a building. These will be the first places to go in a tornado. They will also be the places smoke rises to in a fire, and the fire department will be more than likely spraying down the roof of the building in a fire, so water damage will happen to the servers. This isn't to say that nothing will happen on the bottom floor or in the secure bunker at the school, but it is a way to try to protect the assets you have from storms or other events.

When you do back things up, make sure there is a daily schedule to do that. I personally would look into a twice-a-day schedule, but that might not be possible. The tornado hit in the early evening and most backups happen overnight. So, all of that day's information would have been lost without being backed up. If you do a daily backup, you would have only lost one day's worth of information.

You should also avoid relying on people to backup their own computers and systems when possible. They will forget and so that backup system would have been pointless since it wasn't used.

Student and staff lists are important lists to have backed up off-site regularly. These can be stored in a cloud system, secure server, or even in a part of your student information system, but there needs to be some list of students and staff updated and stored in a secure location. You will need this if you are trying to account for people and/or contact people.

South Middle School was not a building the district was currently using at the time the tornado struck. However, demolition of the building was slowed since the building was older and issues with asbestos had to be handled.
© *Dustine | Dreamstime.com*

CHAPTER 14:
THE COMMAND CENTER

Predetermine Your Command Center Options

Your command center will be a vital tool in a crisis. Your current central office location will be your first choice since those are usually set up to function well in a crisis. But, what would happen if your central office was gone? Where would you go? You need alternate locations selected before you experience a crisis that requires you to relocate. This relocation can be due to a fire, storm, loss of power, or a flood, so having multiple options is best. When looking at possible locations, consider the following items:

1. Do you have multiple phone lines? One of the major problems at the temporary command center Joplin set up was the lack of phone lines. There were only four phone lines in the building, and when you are trying to contact over 9,000 people in addition to fielding hundreds of inbound calls, that number of lines won't work. So, pick locations that will have as many phone lines as possible. Make sure those lines will work even if the district network goes down and are able to be independent of the district's network if needed.

2. What is your Internet connection? Will it work if more than one building gets damaged? When the tornado went through, it sev-

Joplin Schools' administrative center was heavily damaged in the tornado. It housed district servers and other critical systems, which were not fully functional for weeks. However, district officials were able to get into the basement of the center and run payroll by hooking some systems up to generators the day after the tornado to make sure staff were paid on time to have access to much needed funds.

ered the district's Internet connection, so we were without fast Internet for the longest period of time. Consider a satellite connection in the district or at least in a position to be brought in so that you can have Internet and function. Having a wired connection that is star pattern across your district will help prevent you losing a connection if one part is cut, but that costs a lot of money to complete, so until you get there, have a backup plan. You might even look to see if you have the capability to have a cable line or DSL line run to your command center options so that you can easily plug into them if needed.

3. Plan for backup printers and copiers that are not networked. If your network is down, you can't print. And, you will need to be doing a lot of that in a crisis. Having a few non-networked printers and copiers at each of your command center options or in a secure

location is a great idea.

4. Meeting rooms and temporary departments might have to be established in your command center. Make sure the building you choose has those options so you are not bumping into each other just trying to function.

5. An easily secured entrance and exit will be needed. Your administration needs to have a secure working environment, so being able to either lockdown or control the flow of traffic will be needed. Joplin needed to assign someone to do this one job because of the amount of traffic and people wanting to get in to see Central Office staff. With that, you will also need to have a check-in and check-out system in place.

6. Parking will be important, so choose options that can handle large amounts of traffic. In a major disaster, you will have numerous visits, sometimes by high-ranking officials, and you will need to be able to handle a large traffic load at times.

Once you have your locations, you will need to have supplies there or accessible in the event a crisis causes you to have to implement a command center. In your command center there should be the following things:

1. Backup batteries & chargers for both computers and cell phones. You might want to consider solar chargers for events where power is out for a long period of time.

2. Batteries for various electronics. Rechargable batteries help prevent having to hunt down more batteries if you can just recharge them.

3. Backup cell phones for emergency use. These can be phones that are not used until a crisis. Many cellular phone companies allow you to have these for a few cents a month and only charge you when used. Just make sure you test the phones throughout the year

so you don't find out they are broken when you need them.

4. MiFi units/mobile hot spots/cellular Internet cards are great tools. When the Internet goes out, these are great backup options. They might not work well if cell phone towers have been damaged, but they will be better than nothing.

5. Food. Your central office staff might just have to show up in a hurry. Having some supplies on hand will help until food can be brought in or fixed.

6. Clothing for administrative staff. Depending on the crisis, the Central Office staff might not have a chance to go home for long periods of time, so having extra clothes (mainly shirts) on hand to allow for a change of clothes if needed. It is also a good idea to have clothing with your district logo or name on them for your Central Office team to show a unified or official image of your leadership team in a crisis.

7. Another option might be to work to get a temporary cell phone tower on the school property to help with connectivity. This would have to be arranged between you and the cell phone company, but it would help them and the district at the same time.

As part of your district planning, you need to implement a two-way radio system, if you have not done so already. As part of that system, your staff needs to know what to do when an emergency occurs. Which channel do they use as the emergency channel? Do they need to take the radios home each night? How far is your range and do you need a repeater in the district?

Develop security and crisis materials before a crisis. Printing generic tags that the crisis team can wear to show they belong and have access to areas will save time.

Only approved staff could get through police barriers in Joplin. Having that method of identification developed before a crisis will help reduce confusion. Those badges should be different enough that regular staff IDs will not be confused with them.

Designate A Communication Room

You will need a location for the communication department to function and be able to have some element of privacy. There will be sensitive issues that need to be discussed and issues that the communication team will need to brief people on, so having a location that is probably larger than the normal communication department will be needed.

The communication department will need their own phone lines so that they can field the many media calls that will be coming in. This might not be the case in a smaller crisis, but having phone lines that are free from parents calling in and staff calling out will be important in any situation.

The communication team will also need to include a technology person. We would not have survived if Tracie Skaggs had not brought Marshal Graham with her. He and Jason Cravens were troubleshooting things so we were able to do what we needed to do.

One of the best things that we did was post important phone numbers on the wall by the phone, but kept them hidden from those that didn't need to see them. Too many times you are on the phone and need to direct people to different numbers. This was a quick and easy system to allow that to happen.

You also need to have daily schedules posted on the wall for the communication staff and your key administrators who will be doing interviews or fielding questions. We had press conferences, meetings, and multiple other things that we either had to be at or the administration was supposed to be ready for. You need to be able to see the flow of the day and who is available at what time.

When planning major press events or events where multiple people will need to be interviewed, the grid system mentioned before works well. This allows you to divide up time segments and assign different media to those slots. This way you won't double book someone and can also keep the flow of interviews going smoothly.

Organize, Organize, Organize

In a crisis situation, organize early in each department. You will want to designate people to perform certain duties, and those can be very simple things like organizing notes or lists, because things can get crazy in a hurry. Having one person who is the organizer in each department will help make sure things are handled correctly since it will be chaotic at the beginning. Once the system is in place, you can follow it, but have one person who helps develop it.

Having flip charts to write out information and lists will be a great tool. You will want to have folders on hand and develop inboxes so information does not get lost.

We also found that signs (even handwritten ones) were effective in directing people on what to do and where to put things.

In your organizing, document things. Take photos so you can remember how things looked. Write down notes and keep those so you know motivations or reasons why things were done. We constantly looked back at our notes to remember the "why" behind things, which has helped us more than I thought it would.

Plan For Private Time

Your Central Office for front office staff will bear the brunt of a lot of the crisis situation. But, don't forget that you and they have needs as well.

You will want to set up a time for the command center families to see each other. This can be a dinner meeting or some other time, but they need to be able to see their families, especially in an emotional crisis like Joplin.

Dr. CJ Huff attaches an United States flag to what remains of the flag pole outside of Joplin High School. Dr. Huff felt it was an important symbol to raise to show that Joplin Schools wouldn't let the tornado keep them from starting school on time in August 2011.

The administration team will need time to rest. This could be a staggered time for them to go home and then return or even just sleep on cots in a room that is away from the action. If they do not have time to rest, they will not perform effectively. You might have to make people take this time, but it will be important.

Many emergency personnel use the 12 hours on and 12 hours off system. If you have cross trained people, you can have two shifts of people who can work to make sure the district is running effectively while still giving people time to rest.

The administration team might need time for counseling. As you are working with counselors for your students and building staff, don't forget that the command center staff needs this attention as well. It might be delayed compared to others because they are in "crisis mode" and haven't dealt with their emotions yet, but you need to make sure you meet their mental and physical needs, too. They are so busy taking care of everyone else that they sacrifice themselves, but someone needs to look out for them.

What Do You Do With The Superintendent?

This might sound like a stupid question, but your superintendent will be pulled in several directions and you will need to work to make sure he or she is protected. The superintendent is going to have to make decisions and will be focused in so many different areas that you will need to make sure he/she has extra help. So consider the following things:

1. Get the superintendent a "bat phone" so personal calls can be made. If several people have your superintendent's cell phone number, they will be calling that number. He/she may need to be protected from all of these calls so work can actually get accomplished. So work to protect the "bat phone" number and take away the regular cell phone and assign someone to answer it and take messages. Have this talk before a crisis so you aren't trying to pry

the cell phone away in the middle of a crisis. It might not end well for you.

2. Assign a "handler" to the superintendent and other necessary positions. When people are running around like crazy, assigning drivers and assistants to your key positions will do nothing but help. Your administration team is going to be going from place to place and having to make decisions. If they have a driver to take them from place to place and keep them on schedule, they can be productive and have meetings in the car on the way to the next place. Having someone to make sure that the superintendent was at designated places could not have worked better in Joplin. Dr. Huff needed to be in so many places, that in many instances, time got away from him, which is completely understandable.

Additional Staff & Positions to Consider:

After working through the process of insurance, working with FEMA, and having multiple construction projects, your district will want to consider hiring FEMA and insurance advocates and a project manager.

The experts can handle the processes that you would be going through (federal law and requirements can be tricky), and the project manager can make sure that your interests are being addressed in the projects and can work to come to solutions in many construction situations. Let the professionals do what they know how to do and let them help you.

You may also need to hire or expand your communication and safety staff. These groups will be pulled in so many different directions during these situations that in a long-term recovery situation, extra help might be warranted.

Emergency Gear Kits

Joplin was plagued with severe weather that entire week following the tornado. By that first Monday night, I don't think there was a single media truck in the region that hadn't descended on Joplin. So, being on the communications team, were we out climbing through debris to get to the media. With the rain pouring down and jagged debris with nails and glass all over, I would have given anything for a pair of waterproof work boots and a raincoat. Curt and I left that Monday morning after the tornado in a hurry to get to Joplin so those items weren't on my mind to grab (they are now), but they probably won't be on your mind when a disaster strikes. You won't think, "Wait, a tornado just struck my house or school, I need to go get my work boots." You'll more than likely just go into a disaster mode and just start doing what needs to be done. It's the small details that slip your mind until you need something.

So, develop some kits of supplies and store them in your command center options or other safe locations, which might mean you have a few kits. These kits should include rain coats (think about what you see the reporters wearing during a hurricane), boots, gloves, hard hats, reflective vests, and whatever else you might need to prepare for a crisis in your community. Adjust for events that you are more likely to face like winter weather or hurricanes. I'd even throw in some instant coffee or some snack food just in case. You will also want to have flashlights and head lamps. If you have to tromp through debris and carry stuff or move stuff, you need your hands free. And, just in case, you might have some extra clothes in these kits. You never know what situation you will be in and you might need a change of clothes or at least a new shirt or school polo. There are always extra school shirts from various things. Just keep a collection on hand if possible.

In addition to the gear, you need to have some of the basic supplies to function in a crisis. One of the things that we used the most was note pads and pens. At the very beginning of a crisis you are going to be taking notes and you will be inundated with calls, requests, needs, or whatever else people need to be reminded of. So, plan for that.

You will also want to have copies of forms that you will need. These will more than likely be student contact forms, media request forms, student lists, and your crisis manual, as well as any business forms for purchases and daily operations.

You might even think of storing one of these kits outside the district so you can access it in case something major happens in your district. If something the size or scale of what happened in Joplin happened in my district, we might not be able to set up our command center in the district, so having that kit accessible outside the district would be handy and allow for the command center to be set up quickly.

When Cell Phones Go Bye, Bye.

My cell phone. I am that person who uses his cell phone more than I should. I can't go a few moments without checking it. I am addicted, and I admit it. When I sit and think about how much I use my cell phone, I'm not sure how I get my work done without it. Many of you are probably like that, too.

Now, ask yourself what you would do if your cell phone didn't work. For those of you that just passed out and are picking this book back up, you need to be aware of this. We had a cell phone signal, but we were competing against the thousands of calls that were trying to be handled by the cell towers that were left standing after the tornado, and since the tornado went through the heart of the city, these towers were few and far between. So, when we got a call out, it might be lost or jumbled. We even joked that carrier pigeons might have been a faster method of communication on some days.

Having landlines accessible is an important thing. You might even want to look into some form of satellite communication. Having cell phones labeled as emergency phones from different carriers could be a good plan as well. Just like was stated before, some cell phone carriers have plans where you can have phones that you pay a small fee for each month and are only charged when you use them. We kept fighting for signal each day, and it seemed like one carrier would work better than the other on different days.

Things didn't really start to improve until a week or so in. Now, a tornado like the one in Joplin is not a common event, but in a town half the size of Joplin, a much smaller tornado could take out a lot of the communication systems because of their placement. This will also be true of earthquakes, hurricanes, wildfires, and ice storms.

CHAPTER 15:
DEVELOP A DISTRICT-WIDE STRUCTURE

One of the first things we found to be an issue in Nixa was the fact that, while all buildings had safety plans, those plans varied, and sometimes varied greatly. So, when you asked what a particular drill or procedure looked like at one building, it may have looked similar in some ways and completely different in others. While this worked for those buildings, school buildings have to remember they are not an island; they are a part of a bigger picture.

One of the first major steps we took toward a district-wide structure was when we implemented the incident command structure. This will be addressed in the next chapter, but it is a consistent framework that will allow everyone to be speaking the same language and break down barriers between buildings as well as emergency personnel.

So, while we were reviewing what we currently did, we took the great ideas from the different buildings. This is something you need to make sure you don't lose when you are standardizing things. Think of it as more of the district is a country and each building is a state. Some of the best ideas we have are from our buildings solving problems. We can then implement those great ideas district-wide.

What you do need is a district-wide structure to gather those great ideas. That is where your team comes into play. Since they are a cross section of your district, you are more likely to be able to find those since you have input from all levels. You also need to make sure that your team members are assigned to reach out to various areas and ask questions on how people are solving various issues.

One of the biggest problems schools face is training substitutes. This is especially a problem when every building has different code words or procedures. So, when you develop a district-wide structure, the overall approach is the same, and you can train your substitutes on that structure. When they understand the major parts of the plan, they can make those minor adjustments that happen at each building.

Another benefit for having a district-wide structure is that staff from other buildings can step in if needed. If one building is compromised or the staff are incapacitated, that consistent plan and structure allow for people to know procedures. Contrary to how we practice, the crisis isn't going to happen when everything is perfect. You also have to be prepared for the idea that some of your leadership might not function well in crisis situations. You will see some of your strongest leaders fall apart in situations for a number of reasons. This is no fault to them; they just cannot handle the situation they are in. So, that district wide structure allows for that.

This is also why it is important to practice and practice as much as you can, which will be addressed in Chapter 21. You will be able to put stressors in certain situations which will help your staff prepare during simulations and help build that muscle memory for if and/or when an event happens.

And finally, communication is such a vital part of any emergency, having a district-wide structure allows for things to be the same district wide. You know that when "X" happens then "Y" will go into effect. You can also designate certain communication channels on your school radios in the district to be switched to during crisis events so that you are speaking to your administrators or front office staff all at once.

This picture of a hallway in Joplin High School was taken just two days after the tornado struck Joplin. The school was unsafe and many areas could not be touched until certain insurance procedures. The school eventually developed plans to help return what items they could that were in the impacted buildings to the students.

119

We have also implemented "bat phones" for all of our buildings so that when phone lines are jammed in an event, the schools can still call each other or the central office can call them. The numbers are only given to staff members to keep the numbers from being public. As a reminder, you can call your cell phone company to see if they have a program where you can have phone for just a few cents a month and then are only charged per minute.

Another communication tool we have implemented is a "red phone" in each building. And yes, we did actually purchase red phones with a grant. This is plugged into a non-network phone line. If our district network goes down, so do our phones. So, we needed another way to reach our buildings outside of the cell phones, especially if the cell lines are jammed or taken out (both were the case in Joplin).

Above all, those consistent procedures and a district-wide structure is what keep your district held together. Then you allow for some flexibility. You need to keep terms and actions the same, but things that can be varied at each building still should be if needed.

PART 3: TRAIN

Notes:

CHAPTER 16:
THE INCIDENT COMMAND
STRUCTURE IS YOUR FRIEND

When we first started our safety team at Nixa, our local fire district suggested that we look into the incident command structure (ICS) that emergency management agencies use. Then our local emergency management suggested it. So, we looked into it. We realized that we had to use this structure because Nixa had used Federal funds to build tornado safe rooms. This might be something you want to check on if you have accepted funding from FEMA.

The idea of ICS will be one of the greatest mental shifts in your school district. For too long we have focused on the principal or superintendent being in charge and always plan for that. But, what happens when the principal or superintendent isn't at school that day? The principal can't be in charge if he/she isn't in the building. They are calling the shots blind.

Schools also get into the mentality that they can't do anything unless the principal is there, and then they freeze up when something happens or try to call the principal to get guidance. The school building or district has to be able to run with or without the normal person in charge there.

Schools also run into the problem of getting information from different sources and those sources can conflict. One says to send the bus to the

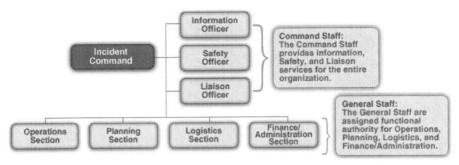

The Incident Command Structure gives your district an organized and consistent format to follow in any situation. Image from training.fema.gov.

school the other still says it is too dangerous. Who should you listen to?

Another issue is that when the emergency personnel show up at your school, they are speaking one language and you are speaking another. Why not have everyone speaking the same language and following the same structure so there are fewer communication issues or decision-making issues?

The ICS switches your command from a person to a position. This means that people assume roles and those roles have defined job responsibilities. It also allows for you to put the best person in each position. If you have a situation that someone has already dealt with before but isn't the "top-level person" in the building or district, it makes perfect sense for that person to be the incident commander.

The system easily breaks down what we already do in schools during a crisis (or at least should be doing), but it allows for flexibility in staffing, takes into account that your leaders aren't always there, and allows those in the situation to still function if the principal or superintendent is absent. Why? Because they all know the structure and can step in as needed.

Nixa had the opportunity to receive training at the national institute in Maryland, which was paid for through grants from FEMA (so you should look into those). We also just happened to be there in the middle of Hurricane Sandy. So, we were able to get a more intimate look at how FEMA works outside of our classroom time by talking to the people there since the training center was a base for deployment.

I also don't think we realized how bad it was in the middle of the storm because we never really lost power. But, we were on a government base that was the staging ground for response, so we really never should have. It wasn't until they let us off base that we saw how much damage was done near us. So looking back at the situation and my decision to stand outside and take video of the storm as it was hitting the base took on a different meaning.

Above all, the ICS is a structure that you can weave into all parts of your school day. That is really what crisis planning is all about. You shouldn't have your normal school day and then have your crisis plans. Your crisis plans and organizational structure should be used at all levels of your school day so everything flows together already before a crisis hits. The ICS structure can be used to plan assemblies or dances or events. It can be the format you use for everything so that more people will know the structure.

CHAPTER 17: CROSS TRAIN PEOPLE

When we arrived in Joplin, we were faced with people who were in shock. They were in a situation that not everyone could mentally handle. I was overwhelmed and I just got there and had no emotional attachment…yet. So, ask yourself, "What would we do if _____ could no longer do his/her job?" Then, fill in the blank with any person. It's a simple question, but in the middle of a crisis, it's one you don't want to be fretting over. Make sure that people that hold key positions in the district or have very specific job assignments cross train people so that others know how to perform their job. This can be as simple as knowing where the shut off valve is to knowing how to run payroll for the district.

This also comes into play with any emergency systems in the district. One person should not know how to do everything. They may be responsible for a lot of things, but knowing how to and having permission to use the communication systems, technology systems, business office systems, and human resources systems, should be a shared responsibility. These systems seemed to be the ones that we used the most at the beginning of the crisis in Joplin. However, you will need people cross-trained in all areas, because each situation is different.

This is also just good practice for an organization. You never know when a car accident, illness, or some other circumstance will pull a person out of a position suddenly, and you need someone that can come in and immediately function in that role and run the basic functions of the position.

One lesson learned in Joplin is that the people who were supposed to be in charge were digging themselves out of the debris as well. Many people who were showing up daily to volunteer no longer had a house or a car or were looking for a family member who was still missing. Some couldn't come into work or get to work. So, people had to still do that job in some fashion. So your people can either be cross-trained now before a crisis or be forced to learn in the middle of one.

As you are cross training people, make sure that you develop checklists for those positions or your vital functions. Those are needed in a crisis, even for those people who have that as their daily job. If you need to step into a position, having that list there to remind you is great. But, when a crisis is going on, even people who perform that duty daily might need it to make sure that they don't miss a step in the middle of the world crashing down around them.

CHAPTER 18:
DON'T FORGET TO TRAIN YOUR STAFF

Building Leadership Teams

One thing Joplin has said all along is that their building teams were a major resource to them throughout the entire situation. They had teachers in addition to administrators on the team and those teams really stepped up to help in the weeks, months, and years after the tornado. These teams met regularly and were easily activated to help guide various events or situations occurring at the buildings. This helped relieve some responsibility from the administration since their duties had to be focused in other areas at times.

Empower Your Staff:

At Nixa, we learned a quick lesson after some initial active shooter trainings: empower your staff to act. We learned that we needed to take it farther after a few security events where the principal wasn't available and a decision had to be made.

So, the first thing to do is empower your staff to act in the best interest of the students in their classrooms. Let them know it is okay to take action to protect their students. If they are acting in good faith, then you'll support them. That basic step will show your trust in them. We have taken that further and held active shooter trainings in our schools and, while not all schools want to do this, we have shown our staff how to fight back if someone breaches the classroom door. If you don't want to do this in your schools, then find some way to empower your staff to act and let them know it is okay to do so.

Then, make sure you empower other staff members to act as needed. We learned that our office staff didn't feel like they had the power or authority to act or make decisions in certain situations. We quickly remedied that. We told them that they could place the building in lock-down if needed. If someone walks in with a gun, they shouldn't have to find the principal. They just need to call for a lockdown.

This can also apply to other situations. It goes back to the "acting in good faith" in emergency or crisis situations to protect the students and staff in the building. If that is the basis for the decision, then they have acted appropriately.

A good question to ask your staff is "What do you not feel you have the power or authority to do in a crisis situation?" Then, see what their answers are and you can help clarify many situations before they even occur.

Plan for Volunteers

In most crisis events, you are going to have people wanting to help. You need a plan now on how you will organize them.

You need clearly defined missions where volunteers can help. They can be short-term or long-term missions, but people will need guidance and you will need control. Things can be simple like stuffing envelopes for a day or cleaning a library.

Above all, document your volunteers and their hours. That is one thing I have heard over and over again is that you need to document your volunteers and their hours because you very well may need that for some report or form or insurance or government document.

Controlling Your Message

As addressed before, during a crisis situation, the information you are putting out from the district is one of the most important things you will be doing to try to stay in control of the situation. However, your staff will be one of the unknown factors in how they will act and react in various circumstances, but addressing some of those early will help to reduce the amount of confusion during an actual event.

- Social media procedures

    - Make sure and discuss with staff what expectations are about posting on social media during a crisis event. They need to understand what they post can have a major impact on the situation. Whether they like it or not, they are an "official school source" and the information they put out will be treated as such.

    - You also need to clarify with them what your social media guidelines or procedures allow and do not allow during school hours. But again, the major thing staff need to realize is the power their words can have during a crisis event and how staying silent sometimes is the best option to keep confusion down and allow the district to focus on the actual situation instead of dealing with rumors from what they have posted. There will already be enough from what your students are posting.

    - In one particular incident in Nixa, I started getting questions from the media about reports coming from our school staff who were posting things on Facebook. The problem was that the information was getting twisted and blown out of proportion. The staff member didn't think about that and was just letting their friends on Facebook know they were okay. However, once the information got twisted (just like it usually will), we started having to take our time to deal with the rumors rather than the actual event, which was a lot less dramatic than it was being made out to be by the rumors.

- Texting during a crisis

  - The same idea of social media posting should apply to texting out to people. What they say will get twisted in some way. It has happened time and time again in multiple situations. I do think that texting is worse because it is like the telephone game. At least with social media many people are seeing the same thing, but with a text message, it can get twisted as it is passed from person to person. So, stress with staff how important it is not to text unless absolutely necessary.

- Central media releases

  - As stated previously, having your information come from one central resource will help reduce confusion. Helping train your staff now on this practice will help keep it consistent in a crisis. This is a simple procedure of discussing how you as a district want information and story ideas shared in normal situations and how that might change in a crisis.

  - Something buildings don't always realize is that the media has limited coverage and has to sift through stories to decide what they will cover. If the district has one focus that it would like out in the media for the week or day, then other press releases on events (as great as the event may be) compete with that. And, if schools are just releasing things that aren't the main focus they can pull attention away from what needs the focus. This will only be made worse in a crisis, so working to have that flow of information from one district source will be a great practice to have as "how you do business."

CHAPTER 19:
DON'T FORGET TO TRAIN YOUR PARENTS

One of the things that schools fear is a crisis happening during school hours. You have hundreds if not thousands of people in one building. And, then you have parents. There is something deep down inside of a parent that floods to the surface when his/her child is in harm's way. I cannot imagine the chaos if the Joplin tornado would have happened during a school day. This is why school was canceled in the south in some places when the string of tornados that hit Tuscaloosa, Alabama rolled through.

But, something is going to happen. It happened in Fair Grove, Missouri, just north of Springfield. A tornado hit during the school day. The roof was ripped off part of the high school and the students had to scramble to other parts of the building or to other school buildings nearby to escape rain and debris.

Then, the wave of parents came. This will always be insanity. What system will you have in place to reunite parents with students? Do they need to go to a certain location? Will you evacuate students from the property? How will you transport them in an evacuation? And, to throw a kink in the plans, you don't always want to publicize your relocation or other safety plans. It's great in a crisis, but what if that

133

crisis involves someone attacking your school in some way. Do you really want everyone to know where you are going to take your students to be "safe"? Weigh the risks and develop some plans, but think it all through.

Parents Need To Know You Have Plans And What to Expect

The main thing you need to do is develop plans. Then do what you can to communicate out that you at least have a plan and how often you practice and other things like that. You want to instill confidence with parents that you care for their children as much as they do.

However, one important thing to communicate out is the fact that parents cannot know all elements of a school's crisis plans, because if they know then the public will know and that would include the "bad guys." This is why districts have to build trust so parents trust them to do what needs to be done to protect their children even if not all of the elements of the plan are known.

Nixa tries to talk about crisis planning a lot. We want parents to know that it is constantly on our minds and a part of everything we do. It's those short reminders as a part of the everyday conversation that helps remind people what you are doing.

Then think of ways you can communicate out various aspects of the plan. Video is great to explain various things like terminology or a highlight of what goes on in a crisis and what parents can expect. That same video can be a checklist for parents to download so they know what plan will be followed. All of this helps parents understand what will be going on.

If you work to communicate that during a lockdown no one gets in or out of a building, that will help you in the middle of a lockdown to reduce the number of parents who show up and try to get in (I can't promise it will prevent all, but you still won't let them in). We had a lockdown situation and parents were banging on the door to be let in.

So, we decided we needed to work to communicate out what happens in a lockdown better. Look for ways in addition to video to communicate our procedures. It could be parent meetings, website pages, or other announcements to help people understand.

This idea can be applied to other aspects like tornados or intruders or relocation plans just so parents have an idea of what their part is in keeping their children safe. Parents have a part, but if you don't let them know what that part is, it is hard for them to play it.

Relocation and Reunification Plans

Communicate now (and again and again) to parents the procedures for relocation. If you can ingrain this in their brains, some of them might remember and wait for directions. We practice fire drills and other emergency situations with our students and staff so they will instinctually know what to do. The same idea has to be in place with parents so they know what to do or what to wait for in an emergency situation.

Irving Elementary was just east of St. John's Hospital and took the full brunt of the tornado. © Kathryn Sidenstricker | Dreamstime.com

Now, this isn't necessarily communicating out all aspects of the plan, but just letting parents know that if something were to happen, they need to know not to come to the school but wait for instructions on what to do. That way, we can return their child to them as soon as possible.

Many do not realize that if we don't know where a student went, we then take resources to look for that child when we could be using those for other things.

While, this will never work perfectly, the more you can communicate and inform, the more parents will feel confident and will work to act appropriately in various situations so you can reunify them with their children.

PART 4: PRACTICE

Notes:

CHAPTER 20:
DRILL, DRILL, AND RE-DRILL

When something happens in a school, everyone wants to know what the school has done to prepare. Having a district-wide schedule of drills for each month is a great template for your district to have. You give schools flexibility on when during the month, but you can make sure that everyone gets those drills that needs to get done accomplished.

You also need to check with local fire code and other codes or state laws to make sure that you are getting in everything you are supposed to. States are passing laws requiring more and more things from schools, so you need to know what you have to do and what is suggested so you can get things in order.

Nixa has developed a form that has each of the required monthly drills for the year so schools know what they have to do each month. This also helps us as a district answer when drills happen in our district.

What you also need to do, as discussed above, is set up consistent procedures for your schools. That way you know that when a drill happens it should look a certain way (adjustments will have to be made for each school, but the overall form looks the same).

When talking about procedures, avoid the TIF. That is a tornado, intruder, and fire drill all back to back at the same time (if you don't have tornado drills, think of the drills that you practice all at the same time). This confuses students when an actual event happens. They should all be their own drill. Now, this does impact instructional time, so you might have to get creative, but avoiding this when possible is great. We have worked to adjust some of our drills so each one can get the focus it needs when we can. Think outside the box. One of those was have talk-through drills.

I guarantee that you don't have drills at your school for every class (especially for junior high and high school). It just doesn't work to have a fire drill every hour of the day. So, if you can plan talk-through drills for all your classes so they go through what to do in their hour. The school procedure stays the same, but, if students know what to do for each hour, it helps with the effectiveness during an actual situation since you've addressed where they go every hour. What this allows you to do is then have more focus on anther drill and doing a full practice while still protecting instructional time.

Try to avoid perfect conditions

While it would be great if a crisis event could happen when everyone was in place during the hour of the day that would cause the least disruption, but that isn't the case. Yet, we practice like that. Work to take the perfection out of the drill and pull people out of the situation who always run things and perform drills outside of the perfect times in the day (lunch, passing time, etc.).

One major issue schools have in the upper grades is trying to have drills that cover all hours. So, why not have talk-through drills at the junior and senior high schools to cover all your hours. If you have a regular drill to establish the overall procedures for your school and then take time in each hour to have teachers discuss what that class would do, you have prepared all hours without having to have a drill every hour of the day. Make sure and talk this idea out with your local fire district or whoever is responsible for overseeing that your school completes the fire drills. We only do this a couple of times a year (once at the beginning of each semester), but it has really been effective.

You should also try and "block exits" by not allowing people to exit their normal way. People need to be able to think on their feet and a fire very well could block the normal exit. This allows people to think through the other options before the real event.

Another way to avoid the perfect conditions is to use surprise drills. While this will freak out some of your schools or principals, this really takes planning outside of the school's hands. We only do one surprise fire drill per school each year at Nixa. This is more for testing the principal's (or the person acting as principal that day) planning since they do the planning of the drills for the school. Just make sure and let the local fire department and your alarm company know that you are doing drills so you don't have everyone show up for a drill.

In those surprise drills, or even in normal drills, you can work with local fire and emergency management agencies to tests the alarm systems and whether or not the alarm notifies everyone in the chain that it should from the fire department to other emergency management agencies. We forget to test this part, but you don't want to figure out that part of the system isn't working during an actual event.

For some of your drills, you may want to bring in local emergency management to help practice. This might be a summer event when school is out to test various parts of your system, but the more you can to do work with your local agencies to practice, the fewer issues you will have in an actual event.

Our nurses have held a drill with local emergency personnel to change the way they triage students, so that when they arrive on site, things are already set up the way the emergency personnel would do it, and students who would need the most attention could get it quickly.

While there are many ways you can remove those perfect conditions in drills, you cannot plan for everything. However, getting people to think outside the box will help you prepare for the unknowns that will happen in any crisis situation.

Joplin High School became a symbol for the district's recovery efforts. After "Joplin" was ripped off of the high school's sign, someone used duct tape to make the word "Hope" and gave the community another motivator to rebuild. Also, local artists used destroyed trees around the high school to carve eagles to watch over the school and city.
© Proseuxomai | Dreamstime.com

CHAPTER 21: FORCED PRACTICES

There are several times we go through events in districts. I like to call those events, forced practices.

For example, we had a gas leak near our central office and early childhood center in Nixa. We were told to get out. So, our evacuation and relocation plans went into effect.

The first problem, we couldn't go to our normal relocation place because it wasn't accessible because of the gas leak. Then we had to make a decision on a secondary location. It was one of those, "call them and tell them we are coming" instead of asking if it was okay. We have a good enough relationship with our city that the place we went was okay, but this situation gave us a lot to think about.

Many of us also realized in that event what we did and did not immediately accessible to us: phone numbers, Internet, our crisis plan, etc. We now have those things in a cloud system and programed onto our phones and tablets and wherever else we can place them.

Then, in another situation, there was the guy on a bike with a gun. This was early on in my public relations career. We had someone who rode by one of our schools with what appeared to be a gun. He was visited by our city police, school resource officers, the county sheriff, and, I'm pretty sure, the Missouri Highway Patrol. We had schools in lockdown, but it was right at the beginning of the school day, so parents were dropping students off.

So, what do you do? What is the best way to notify people? This is where texting is a great feature to have. I wish we would have had it because we had to send out several rapid notification calls in succession and the information was overwhelming to parents at that point in time. It also taught us how to communicate out information quickly and clearly. And, once the situation was resolved, it was found it was just part of a gun that he found at a garage sale. Another lesson learned: don't ride by a school with any part of a gun clearly displayed...people will freak out.

And, then there was a friend of mine who had a lot of rumors going on in her school district. So, they released a statement that had the words "rumors of violence" in the first sentence. The rest of the statement clarified that there was no violence and never was going to be. The students had planned a flash mob, but many parents didn't read past the first sentence because they just saw the words "violence" and stopped reading.

So, learn how to word certain things so you don't cause people to stop reading before they should. Also, realize that a majority of people will not read past the first paragraph or two of what you put out. So, put what you want to communicate in the first part and then plan for that being all they will read. Then expand on that main point in the rest of the information.

We also had a lockdown because of a police chase around a few of our buildings. Our schools were told to go into a modified lockdown. Well, one school went into full lockdown with lights off, shades drawn, and everyone quiet. Another school just secured outside entrances and kept the daily activities more normal. Who was wrong, well, neither to a certain extent. We needed to clarify what they were supposed to do, so we developed a "secure mode" and a "lockdown"

144

mode for schools to clarify exactly what should be done, and we eliminated a "modified lockdown" from our practice. We also learned what staff needed/wanted during a lockdown event as far as information. While you may not have anything new to share, just sending out an update to let them know that nothing is new will help them feel less isolated and making sure they know when the next update will come and how it will come will help keep them from feeling abandoned and alone.

We also learned that our staff are able to do what needs to be done. When a school is in lockdown for over an hour, you have to be creative, especially if you teach kindergarten. After the situation ended, my favorite story came from a parent of a kindergarten student who came home talking about how much fun they had the afternoon of the lockdown. His class had "silent movie day" where they got to sit on the floor and watch a movie but had to be quiet and make up the story in their heads. And that, my friends, is how it's done!

Looking toward the St. John's Hospital campus, one could see the remains of what used to be multi-story buildings that were reduced to piles of rubble just a few feet high. © *Proseuxomai | Dreamstime.com*

145

From these events as well, we reminded staff that during security events, they should not text out or post on social media. Rumors were getting started when they were doing that and it ended up causing us to have to start dealing with those more than facts in a few situations.

These are just a few examples of our "forced practices," and there are many more lessons learned from them. So, when small events happen, learn from them. They will help point out holes in your plans or areas you haven't addressed.

PART 5: REVIEW AND REPEAT

Notes:

CHAPTER 22: DEBRIEF

Debriefing is the one thing I am horrible at. I know it and own it, but it is the one thing that can be a gold mine of information.

Even after a small event, take a few moments to debrief. If it is a larger event, plan a formal debriefing session. But no matter what, get feedback. You can easily debrief with a short faculty meeting before or after school or send out an email asking for feedback. Some situations will require a more formal debriefing, but you will always want to ask for feedback. Never be afraid that it will show an inadequacy on the part of your leadership in the school. Take it as an opportunity to learn how to make your building plans better.

When we had an event at one of our schools that involved us quarantining a certain part of the school, we learned that while we felt we were doing a good job of informing staff, they didn't feel the same way. We also learned other things that we needed to change. We took this list and that helped us adjust. It also gave our staff a chance to be heard because they saw the same event from many different perspectives.

In an ongoing crisis, make sure you plan for regular debriefings (daily or more as the situations requires) and make sure ALL leadership team members are debriefed so you can see who needs what and make sure you keep mental health services provided in an ongoing fashion. Some businesses or schools have mandated a weekly meeting with a mental health professional for a certain time after a crisis just to make sure that there is someone there to listen. I know that I didn't fully process what I went through in Joplin until at least a month later and I needed to talk it out. Every person will process the situation differently.

Another thing we did learn was to take notes on things as they happen whenever possible or make yourself sit down each night and review the day and what you learned or forgot or needed to change. Things will be happening so quickly and it will be a crazy time that the notes you take along will be a wealth of information when you need to review what happened.

We did this in the middle of the craziness in Joplin. We all sat around Tracie's table at her house and just tried to take notes on everything each night. I think together we had a complete list of what went on. That also allowed us to just talk and laugh and cry and decompress and get things out of our minds. I think our minds just need to dump all the information out sometimes before we can rest. And resting is what will keep your leadership team going.

Those notes are what developed into this book. Without those, I don't think we could have fully covered everything. When you read back through the notes you remember what happened, but many times we forgot about events or things that we needed to review until we reviewed the notes. These notes can also help as people switch shifts if your event requires people to be around for a large chunk of the day or rotate duties off and on for different days of the week. The person leaving can brief the person coming in and leave details on what was going on so everyone can be on the same page. They can also be used to refer back to when you need to remember things.

CHAPTER 23:
YOU'LL NEVER BE DONE, AND IT'S OKAY

One of the hardest lessons I have had to learn with crisis planning is that you'll never be done. Ever. And, that's okay.

There will always be something new to address. A new crisis will happen. That's where the team structure comes in. Have a regular update schedule and pull your team together to review things. Our team in Nixa meets quarterly. At the beginning, we were meeting for several hours. Then, as we progressed into more of a groove of how we do business, our meetings were able to be shorter.

However, writing a crisis plan is the area where many schools stop. Some move on to the review stage, but they don't apply what they learn. After some crisis event (either local or national), there is a treasure trove of information that is released that you can use to see how you measure up in your district.

After the Sandy Hook shooting, our crisis team met and reviewed district procedures and went through every email that parents and the community sent in with questions or suggestions. We were able to adjust things where we could and also take a comprehensive look at what we do. What we found is that we had in place many things that experts credited for slowing down the shooter. That helped us reinforce what we were doing. It was also the time for us to make changes

151

because people were more open to adjusting some procedures.

Every event is a time to look at what happened and what we can learn from it, even events that don't involve schools. A lot was learned from the Boston bombing. One major lesson was how the Boston Police Department utilized Twitter to send out information quickly as well as dispel rumors that were going around. They were able to correct rumors or false information quickly. For schools scared of jumping into social media, Twitter might be a great first step and also develop a way to communicate information out quickly in a crisis at the same time. However, this should be set up now so you are not scrambling to do it in the middle of a crisis.

The shooting at a school in Nevada showed us that schools with lockdown plans that work help prevent students from getting into the building. While lives were lost in that event, we see how plans put into place can be effective.

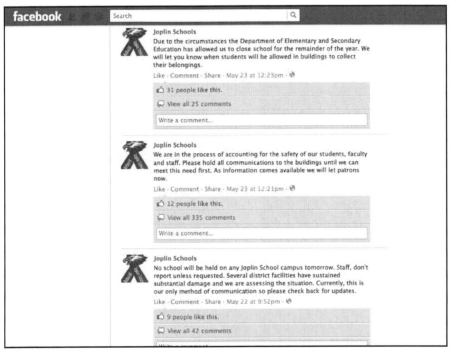

The Joplin Schools Facebook page became the central hub of information just like Twitter did during the Boston bombing.

So learn to plan. Learn to learn from other events. And, plan to develop a structure so that you can review and revise plans as needed and never make a knee-jerk reaction without studying what actually happened.

PART 6: OTHER LESSONS

Notes:

CHAPTER 24: CELEBRATE

In the midst of the hell that was the Joplin tornado, there was one thing Dr. Huff made everyone do. We celebrated things every day. This is a very important thing to do.

In the middle of the chaos and being completely overwhelmed, each day we could see a little ray of sunshine. It could be that we just got an email sent or put up signage, but we celebrated.

This mentality carried on throughout that first summer and even to this very day. When you only focus on the negative you forget the good things. And, in a crisis event, there are going to be so many bad things draining you both mentally and physically that you need the good things.

You may need to have a wall that has your things that you need to do on paper and then move those to a new wall when they get completed. It is just a way to show you are moving forward and are in a better spot that you were the previous day.

You could also have a wall of celebrations where staff can write positive things to be posted on a wall. Some schools have even carried this idea to their schools throughout the year by having a "hidden hero" wall where people write down cool things others are doing to make the

Dr. Huff holds a rally at Joplin High School to help celebrate the successes that the district had made in just a few days, but he also used it as a time to encourage staff and let them know that Joplin Schools was going to make it through the recovery together and come out stronger.

school a better place.

Another thing to remember is that, while something might not be a big deal to you, it might be a big celebration for a building or a particular group in your district and it should be celebrated, especially in the middle of a crisis like Joplin.

Too many times in a crisis we just get to checking things off the to-do list because we have so much going on. But, stopping to celebrate can remind you that you are making a difference. These are also opportunities to invite your community in to celebrate with you. You have groups of people who have been working to fix things or clean or just remove debris. They should be recognized and celebrated. This can help rally people

No matter what you do, keep positive things in the mix because the negative will overrun you if you don't.

CHAPTER 25:
SECURE YOUR PROPERTY

One issue that many of us did not even think about was securing the district property. Our focus was on finding students and getting a handle on the situation, not putting up a fence. This is something that needs to happen as soon as possible when a building is damaged. Assign a team to deal with human needs and assign others to deal with property needs.

First, you need to keep people out of areas that are not safe. One of your biggest problems will be keeping staff out of the buildings. They will want in to get their stuff, and this can be a hazardous situation for them. You don't want them doing this because it can cause issues with insurance companies. Plus, the building could collapse on them. You will also have to deal with theft and others just going into places in the building that they shouldn't be. It happens in every crisis event: Hurricane Sandy and Katrina to earthquakes and other events that leave buildings exposed. People go in and steal and schools can be ripe targets for that.

So, as soon as possible, get a fence up around the property and post "Private Property" and "No Trespassing" signs. Know which buildings have asbestos issues and post those signs as well. Then use your school resource officers to help with security at damaged buildings. If you do not have SRO's in your district or the situation pulls your

Securing your school property with a fence or other barrier should be a top priority to help protect your property as well as prevent injuries from people going into unsafe buildings.

SRO's into other positions or situations, consider hiring a security company to come in and help. There are a lot of valuable things in schools and you can't get it all out of the buildings quickly in most instances.

One thing to consider is letting everyone know a building is dangerous yet still posting pictures of people in that building or in the building without hard hats and proper safety equipment. People will think you were lying to them and not obey your "keep out" direction. You are leading the district, so you have to follow your own safety messages.

CHAPTER 26:
DON'T FORGET WHAT IS MOST IMPORTANT...PEOPLE

In the middle of the craziness in a crisis, many times we get focused on the checklist of things and forget about the people. But people are not and should never be a checklist. Don't ever lose sight of that fact.

During the first part of the recovery process, Joplin employed floating subs that were available to take over a class for an hour or two if a staff member needed to go sign some paperwork or have an appointment with their doctor or insurance agent.

First, it didn't seem to be good to have teachers taking off half-days all the time just to go take care of things quickly. Many staff would have used all of their time off in just a few months when it wasn't needed. Other times, staff just got overwhelmed and need to step out of class. After a major event, each person processes the event differently and some people don't process it for weeks or months. This might be the case after another situation like the death of a student or staff member.

Joplin also looked beyond the students and staff and looked at the whole families. They planned camps during breaks (winter/Christmas, spring break, and summer) so that parents wouldn't have to worry as much about childcare. Many local groups stepped up to help out with these camps as well. There is nothing like losing everything and then

With only weeks left of summer and many of Joplin Missouri's school buildings either destroyed or severely damaged by the Massive EF-5 tornado that ripped through their town on May 22, 2011, school children faced an uncertain future. © Dustine | Dreamstime.com

trying to find money to pay for childcare when school isn't in session. That first summer it really allowed parents to have a place for their children while they were going through the pile of debris that used to be their house.

During those camps, students also had access to school services. Counselors (both school counselors and others who came to help) could continue to work with students who needed extra attention. Students were also guaranteed meals during those camps. In a town with a high free or reduced lunch rate, making sure students had food not only helped their recovery, it also helped parents who were digging out of the storm.

The camps were also a great way for people in the community to volunteer, but you can also plan to pay staff who are trying to rebuild. Many times businesses and organizations will help sponsor these events.

Dr. Huff has always said that he was and still is inspired by how the students responded. Never underestimate youth. He said they are profound and resilient and will surprise you if you give them the chance. And, by Joplin focusing on them, the district set their students up to be able to receive the assistance they needed and work to recover from the tragedy that they went through. While many people worried that students wouldn't show up at school the first day, almost all who were supposed to be there did. Joplin made their schools a safe place to heal after the storm and made it okay for students to process what had happened to them.

CHAPTER 27: TELL YOUR STORY

As I said before, if you always realize there is a story to tell, you will always work to find that. And that is what Joplin did. Joplin did that in a way that I really had never seen and haven't really seen since.

If you look at the number of videos the district produced of the security footage and their recovery efforts, it will astound you. I firmly believe that is one of the reasons they received the outpouring of support they did. They didn't let others tell their story, they told it themselves. They showed how their students were doing. They showed recovery efforts and kept the narrative of their story out front.

They also kept the visual narrative going by showing photos of recovery efforts and donations and other things going on. In that first week, we worked to give specific visuals to show that Joplin wasn't beaten--they were just bruised and they would rise from the debris.

The "Beat the Clock" logo was developed and donated by Jeremy Bartley.

That is also where the idea of "Operation Rising Eagle" came into effect and the "Beat the Clock" to the first day of school came into play. When you have a clear deadline and you rally people to meet it, you give them a common purpose and a goal. And, I think people like a challenge.

The "Beat the Clock" idea came after Dr. Huff made the decision that Joplin would open on schedule in August. We had a logo donated and to kick it off, we found one of the countdown clocks that had been used to countdown to the football season. Walking past that every day was a reminder to everyone of the approaching deadline and the job we had to do for the students of Joplin.

"Operation Rising Eagle" was what Joplin named their efforts to rebuild and recover as a school district. It was also a way for people to rally and have a clear and focused purpose to help Joplin recover. When you can funnel your efforts together and show the results of those efforts through photos and video, people will keep supporting them.

Now, as the district opens buildings, they are working to keep their

When teachers and staff came back to work the August after the tornado, the community of Joplin rallied and lined the streets and sidewalks to cheer for them.

166

story alive by giving people tours of the buildings and showing progress of the rebuilding efforts.

You need to work to have your communication avenues set up before a crisis happens. This will help you already have the channels established to tell your story. And, you need to make sure your channels evolve as your audience does. For example, an October 10, 2013 article from Poynter showed that 34% of Millennials mainly watch videos online. So, as your next group of parents come along, if you don't have video you aren't reaching them effectively, and you have to reach your entire demographic in order to tell your story effectively.

This story-telling process will always evolve and change and could very well be different in your district, so be proactive in developing your channels for telling your story so that when you need to tell it you can.

CHAPTER 28:
THE AIR STILL FEELS WEIRD

On the morning of October 18, 1984, as my family walked outside, I remember my mom saying how the air felt "weird." At 5:10 p.m., when the wall clock stopped and the front doors were sucked open, our lives were changed forever, in just the blink of an eye.

It's funny how a memory like that is ingrained in your mind and your senses forever. I still feel a little twinge when the air has that same strange sense, and I guess I always will. It's something I won't forget, and, in some way, I don't want to, because I am reminded that I can overcome what life throws at me.

The people of Joplin will forever be in my heart. I know that when the sky goes dark they will be reminded of that fateful evening. But, if they remember to look around them they will see a community that has stood tall and strong because they did it together, and that can be their inspiration to keep going.

ABOUT THE AUTHOR

Zac Rantz is a native of Nixa, Missouri, and works at the director of communication for Nixa Public Schools. Prior to his current position in the district, he taught English and journalism at Nixa High School.

He is active in several community organizations and has held leadership positions in the Missouri School Public Relations Association (MOSPRA), including serving as its president.

Zac is also speaker at local, state, and national conferences as well as marketing classes and administration certification classes.

Zac obtained his Bachelor's in secondary English education and Master's in Integrated Marketing Communication from Drury University.

For his work in communications, he has been recognized with the following awards "20 Under 30" for 417 Magazine, "Rookie of the Year" for MOSPRA, "Men of the Year" from the Springfield Business Journal, "35 Under 35" in the nation for the National School Public Relations Association, and the 2014 national "Leadership Through Communication" award from the American Association of School Administrators and the National School Public Relations Association.

For more information, go to www.zacrantz.com.

Made in the USA
Lexington, KY
12 March 2014